Numerology for Beginners

How to Discover Yourself and Understand Others Through Horoscope, Tarot, Numerology, Zodiac Signs and Wicca

(Become a Master at Fortune Telling Using Proven Math)

Dan Bauer

Published by Rob Miles

© **Dan Bauer**

All Rights Reserved

Numerology for Beginners: How to Discover Yourself and Understand Others Through Horoscope, Tarot, Numerology, Zodiac Signs and Wicca (Become a Master at Fortune Telling Using Proven Math)

ISBN 978-1-989990-43-8

All rights reserved. No part of this guide may be reproduced in any form without permission in writing from the publisher except in the case of brief quotations embodied in critical articles or reviews.

Legal & Disclaimer

The information contained in this book is not designed to replace or take the place of any form of medicine or professional medical advice. The information in this book has been provided for educational and entertainment purposes only.

The information contained in this book has been compiled from sources deemed reliable, and it is accurate to the best of the Author's knowledge; however, the Author cannot guarantee its accuracy and validity and cannot be held liable for any errors or omissions. Changes are periodically made to this book. You must consult your doctor or get professional medical advice before using any of the suggested remedies, techniques, or information in this book.

Upon using the information contained in this book, you agree to hold harmless the Author from and against any damages, costs, and expenses, including any legal fees potentially resulting from the application of any of the information provided by this guide. This disclaimer applies to any damages or injury caused by the use and application, whether directly or indirectly, of any advice or information presented, whether for breach of contract, tort, negligence, personal injury, criminal intent, or under any other cause of action.

You agree to accept all risks of using the information presented inside this book. You need to consult a professional medical practitioner in order to ensure you are both able and healthy enough to participate in this program.

Table of Contents

INTRODUCTION 1

CHAPTER 1: NUMEROLOGY 4

CHAPTER 2: PINNACLES AND UNDERTONES: 18

CHAPTER 3: WHAT IS NUMEROLOGY? 27

CHAPTER 4: DESTINY NUMBER 45

CHAPTER 5: THE SPIRITUAL ANGLE TO NUMEROLOGY 53

CHAPTER 6: MEANING OF BIRTH DATE NUMBERS 64

CHAPTER 7: WHAT YOUR EXPRESSION NUMBER SAYS ABOUT YOU 80

CHAPTER 8: UNDERSTANDING NUMBERS AND DIGITS 89

CHAPTER 9: IF YOU BORN ON THE 5 (FIFTH) OR 14TH (FOURTEENTH), OR 23RD (TWENTY THIRD) OF ANY MONTH THAN KINDLY 98

CHAPTER 10: NAME (OR EXPRESSION) NUMBER 111

CHAPTER 11: KARMIC DEBT NUMBERS 120

CHAPTER 12: COMMON MISTAKES 135

CHAPTER 13: WHAT TYPE OF LIFE-MATE ARE YOU. 144

CHAPTER 14: THE COSMIC CLOCK OF LEO 150

CHAPTER 15: TIPS WITH NUMEROLOGY 170

CHAPTER 16: EXPRESSION NUMBER 174

CHAPTER 17: WARNING NUMBERS 187

CHAPTER 18: THE MOON... 192

CONCLUSION... 204

Introduction

In simple terms, numerology is a study of numbers in your life. You can uncover information about the world and also each individual person by using Numerology. Numerology is seen as a universal language of numbers.

If you are familiar with Astrology, then you may know a little bit about Numerology; it is similar in quite a few ways, but uses a different method to get the information and insight: Numbers.

Numerology is the idea that the universe is a system and once broken down, we are left with the basic elements, which is numbers. These numbers can then be used to help us to better understand the world and ourselves as individuals.

Numerology is the idea that the universe is a system; once broken down, we are left with the basic elements, which is numbers. By understanding that everything in the world is dependent on, and can equate to numbers, a numerologist can take multiple elements of a person and break them down into meaningful numbers through various methods. These numbers can then be used to help us to better understand the world and ourselves as individuals where you can discover insights about your purpose and personality traits by working out things like your life path number, expression number and heart's desire number among many others.

Numerology is the study of numbers and how they form a specific vibration. Every name holds a vibration which means that every name has a unique set of characteristics. Many people think that numerology holds no meaning and they classify it with tarot cards and the occult.

Numerology is very accurate when properly interpreted. We can analyse well know people and take advantage of hindsight in determining their primary numbers for their names and birth date and applying these to their lives.

Even if we do not see numbers as somewhat mystical forces, we can realize that numbers keep coming to our life and play a vital role in determining our life path. Right from the day we come into this world to the day we take our last breath, every moment of our life can be defined in terms of numbers. This precise quality of numbers is what makes them extra special to the students of metaphysics. Numbers have such a significant meaning and hints that it is all but natural for all of us to make the study of them a compulsory part of our life.

Chapter 1: Numerology

Numerology has been used for centuries as a means to access the divine through the use of numbers. Seeing natural patterns in numbers and recognizing their influence is a big part of this practice. As you begin this journey be aware of the patterns around you in everyday life. It is one thing to use numbers as a means of measuring or counting, but to see their presence in all aspects of life takes a heightened awareness and great observation skills.

What is Numerology?

Numerology techniques can be used for a multitude of various reasons. Some use the patterns in numbers to make decisions about investments and to draw scientific influences from the numbers. Some may use the patterns to analyze the economy and its ups and downs over a long period of time. For our intents and purposes in this book, we use the traditional definition of numerology as it was used by mystics and students long ago, as a way to build relationships with numbers as a means to connect with the divine. This belief adheres to the idea that there is an inherent mystical relationship between numbers and certain events that take place around the world as well as in our personal lives. These studies also believe that there is a mystical numerical value to many things including; words, names, thoughts, planets and individuals themselves.

Within these esoteric beliefs, it is thought that there are only nine numbers. 1,2,3,4,5,6,7,8, and 9 are thought to be the only actual numbers that exist, while any number 10 and above is simply the base nine numbers repeating themselves. This is seen by the simple act of taking the number 10, adding its digits together (1+0=1) and having a sum of 1. If you were to continue, you would see that each subsequent number adds up to the pattern of 1, 2,3,4,5,6,7,8 and 9.

Example: Eleven; 1+1=2, Twelve; 1+2=3, Thirteen; 1+3=4

This pattern carries on infinitely. And this technique is the very basic principle of numerology; adding digits together to receive a single digit value. While numbers with more than one digit do have their complex personalities on their own, by reducing the value down to one digit, we can see its most basic aspects. You can essentially take any number and reduce them to a single digit using this technique and have meaningful insight into what that number may mean to you or the greater world.

This brings up the question of zero as well. In many numerological systems, zero is not considered a number. It is thought of as infinite, rather than having a value. Zero has no beginning or end; it is empty. While zero is still used to symbolize value, it needs another number before it to have any value at all. This is why zero is left out of the base numbers, and of course, when reducing numbers to single digits zero is zero.

The actual use of the word numerology is fairly new. Dating back to as early as 1907 in the English language, numerology was popular during the Victorian era in the western world, but we see with is expansive history that numerology has been practiced for centuries, potentially even before the use of writing. With more recent surges in popularity, numerology has a history and contemporary power that is validated more so each day with its successful use.

This study of numbers reveals to us the habits and tendencies of our personality. We can also apply this to other's personalities. The numbers reflect a certain pattern that we seem to naturally adhere to. It is thought that the vibrations of certain sounds have a numerical value, and since life is a series of vibrations every event potentially can be attributed to a number. As far as your personal numerology these numbers will reveal an exceptional amount of detail about your purpose in life, your aspirations, and how you may find your true calling. Numerology can be used to time big events in life, or better prepare for them as well. With all the wonderful uses many feel like it is too good to be true or too complicated. It may seem complex, but most things in life are. Whether you're trying to become an expert in numerology or just want to improve a few aspects of your life, it is good to consider its history and use.

Historical use of numerology

We know that numerology has been practiced for centuries, but we can't quite pinpoint its exact beginnings. Like so many other esoteric and occult practices it is impossible to know its exact origin, but we can analyze our earliest records of numerology. It is to be expected that we find these techniques used in early civilizations. There has been evidence discovered in written records of the use of numerology in Egypt. Even earlier we see that the Chaldean system of Babylon uses numerology. Experts agree that the Chaldean system was greatly influenced by Hebrew numerology. More recent use of numerology has been discovered in China and Japan dating back just a few thousand years.

While these old civilizations were using numerology, it is tough to know how broad the scope of their studies actually was. Modern-day numerology is often attributed to the writings of the popular Greek philosopher Pythagoras. Pythagoras' work with numbers and mathematics have influenced modern day use in an incredible way. His ideas that numbers were an important role in any event or relationship have formed mathematical thought to what it has become today. Pythagoras felt that it was the duty of the mind to contemplate the numerical relationships between all things.

As time went on and the influence of Christianity spread rampantly across the western world, certain practices were condemned, including numerology. Numerology, along with astrology and tarot, were classified as magic and considered to be evil practices. This religious suppression of the magical arts created a huge shift in the use of numerology. Many were forced to work in private or be subject to the influence of numbers without even knowing it. Even though the power of the church did well in eliminating numerology practices, the Bible itself has heavy use of numbers and numerological practices. It is safe to say that the influence of numbers is unavoidable.

We can learn a lot about the popular history of numerology, but we learn even more by analyzing how numerology was used in different cultures. One of the more common practices using numbers to assign a value to certain sounds or letters of the alphabet. This is found in many ancient cultures, notably in Kabbalah and the Hebrew language where the symbol's numerical value is just as important as the sound it makes when spoken. There are many differing opinions about how these different systems are translated into English with their numerical value. Below are some examples of alphabets and their numerological values.

Latin Alphabetic Values

1 – a, j, s   2 – b, k, t   3 – c,l,u

4 – d,m,v   5 – e, n, w   6 – f, o, x

7 – g, p, y   8 – h, q, z   9 – i, r

Indian or Vedic Alphabetic Values

1 – a, l, j, q, y   2 – b, k, r   3 – c, g, l, s

4 – d,m, t   5 – e, h, n, x   6 – u, v, w

7 – o, z   8 – f, p   9 – i, r

Pythagorean Alphabetic Values

1 – a, j, s   2 – b, k, t   3 – c,l,u

4 – d, m, v   5 – e, n, w   6 – f, o, x

7 – g, p, y   8 – h, q, z   9 – i, r, x

These two systems are the most common systems that have been translated into English. Other languages rely heavily on the sounds themselves and are more complex than the English alphabet; this makes it difficult to account for sounds that are found in English but not in other languages and vice versa. Also, the use of numerical values is different in many languages, based more on the sounds and other qualities like whether or not the word is a homophone or has other attributes, like an unlucky history or connotation.

We see other attributions as well besides alphabets. Assigning numbers to the planets and other heavenly bodies is a very popular idea found in many cultures as well. These numerical values are not all identical across the board though. Below are numerical values found in Indian or

Vedic numerology, as well as Kabbalah numerology.

The numbers Indian

1 - Sun

2 - Moon

3 - Jupiter

4 - Rahu

5 - Mercury

6 - Venus

7 - Ketu

8 - Saturn

9 – Mars

Kabbala

1. The Sun

2. The Moon (New)

3. Jupiter

4. The Earth or Sun

5. Mercury.

6. Venus

7. The Moon (Full)

8. Saturn

Tree of life

1 - Pluto

2- Uranus

3 - Saturn

4 – Jupiter

5 - Mars

6 - Sun

7- Venus

8 - Mercury

9 – Moon

10 – Earth

So we see here how the numerical value of certain things can be viewed through many lenses. Depending on the context these values can be used successfully. There is no one way to view the numbers; they exist on levels even beyond our perspective as humans in modern times. It is wise to use a numerology system that feels right to you. Pick a system that may be in line with your ancestry or whichever one may be the most attractive to you.

Contemporary use of numerology

Today numerology is used by a wide variety of people in many different forms. We see spiritually minded people as well as the less spiritually inclined building new relationships with numbers and their natural influence. There is a popular uprising of occult practices which has led to numerology's modern acceptance as well. New age groups, occultists, neo-pagans, and even atheists have all found members of their respective perspectives using numerology and astrology to improve their lives and develop a new understanding as to the true nature of reality. Even more traditional religious sects still use ancient numerology practices in their daily lives.

It is also common in our technologically advanced world to really question how numerology may work. While there is very little investment in trying to validate these practices, you will find very few studies to attempt to. The mysterious nature of these esoteric ideas and practices is something that was of no concern to students in ancient times. If the techniques worked then, that was proof enough. When developing a worldview that is trying to fit the validity of numerology into its philosophy be open minded.

Many believe the numbers themselves to have life and power, whether in our world or another. Some feel that the number's power comes from complex patterns that are built into nature and affect us that way. Others still feel there is spiritual intelligence that works through numbers to communicate with us. However, you want to explain your work to keep in mind that no one really knows for sure.

While many people have had fun calculating their personal numerology online, rarely does their practice go beyond this small venture into onto the numerology path. It is fun to memorize your personal numbers, but actually working with them is where the real empowerment comes into play. Not unlike someone stating their astrological sun sign, "Oh I'm a Pisces so …" many do the same with their personal numerology.

It is recommended that if you are taking a serious approach to empowering yourself through numerology that you refrain from getting caught up in vague understandings and umbrella terms. If you truly wish to gain insight from these practices it is best suggested that you approach them with humility and focus on what actually works for you rather than what's popular in our society. No one system or technique will work for everyone, find your style and niche and use it. With this in mind let's move onto how to calculate your personal numerology.

Chapter 2: Pinnacles And Undertones:

1st Pinnacle: **3** (month + day)
1st Undertone: **4** (month - day or day - month)

2nd Pinnacle: **4** (day + year)
2nd Undertone: **5** (day - year or year - day)

3rd Pinnacle: **7** (1st + 2nd Pinnacles)
3rd Undertone: **1** (1st - 2nd Pinnacle or 2nd - 1st Pinnacle)

4th Pinnacle: **8** (month + year)
4th Undertone: **1** (month - year or year - month)

Reminder: all calculations are either adding or subtracting one from the other

Personal Year: the sum of the 1st Pinnacle and the current year. In the example above, the Personal Year is a 6.

Façade: the sum of the entire birth date. In the above example, the Façade is a 3. In other systems of numerology, this is referred to as the Life Path. This how others see you and the side you show to the world.

Pinnacles are the strong influences that guide daily life. This includes personality, how a person thinks and acts. This sets the mood and predicts one's behavior.

Undertones are the events, people, circumstances and emotions that surround a person. Undertones are the reaction, the outcome of a sequence of life events.

Birthday and Facade Numbers: The Outer Self Vs the Real Personality

August 13, 1927

8 + 4 + 1 = 4 Façade

To create the basic framework for analyzing someone's birthday, write out the day of birth. Below the month, day, and year, sum up the numbers to a single digit. Keep in mind that adding any number with 9 will total to the other digit, so leave out 9 and combinations of 9, such as 1 + 8, 2 + 7, 3 + 6, as well as 4 + 5. Place the single digit total of all these numbers, the Façade, to the right of the set. Some numerologists refer to the Façade number as the Birth Path or Destiny number, and they claim this to be the number that governs one's life. However, analyzing by the Birth Path number is analogous to deciding someone's basic astrological make up by the sun sign alone. No astrologer worth his salt will emphasize the sun sign alone without considering the rest of the natal chart. He'll look at the ascendant, placement of the planets in the houses, aspects, the Midheaven, and so forth. Therefore, I call this general number the Facade because it reflects the personality that others see.

I look at the day of birth first and last. It tells me the individual's "dharma," the Sanskrit word for general personality and essence. The façade number is a good indicator of how one comes across to others. The façade is the outer being, whereas the Birthday number always will be the final indicator of one's real and intrinsic nature.

I use the number value of the day of birth to analyze basic character, personality, one's general life view, and the way in which he deals with his environment. The general effects of the Birthday number increase when it is the same as the Façade number. The above example is the number make up of Fidel Castro, the socialist dictator of Cuba. The Façade and the Birthday numbers match, so Castro never shows himself to be something he isn't. He is a good example of a like Facade number increasing the tendencies of the Birthday, for he is both a 4 Facade and a 4 Birthday. Prime characteristics of 4 Birthdays are that of being firm, dependable, and exacting, but also stubborn and controlling. 4s are at their best as big fish in a small pond. They also prefer to work side-by-side with those they supervise. During the Bay of Pigs invasion, Castro led a company of troops into battle and, in his younger days, he occasionally joined the peasants in harvesting sugar cane. Castro is world renowned for tight political control over his personal island and always has been firm and exacting with his subordinates. He can be depended on to keep a hard socialistic political line while the world Communist bloc has fallen apart.

Comparing the Façade and Birthday numbers will show you why an individual comes across differently interpersonally than what he or she shows up front. The further apart the Façade and the Birthday numbers, the more easily they appear as so-called "two-faced." A 7 Birthday's withdrawn nature increases with the 7 Façade number, but the serious 7 Birthday might seem more playful and sociable if his Façade is a 3. A 2 Birthday is more indecisive if its Facade and Birthday are both a 2, but will appear more decisive and in control of himself if his Facade is a 4 or an 8. An individual has to deal with feeling at odds with himself if his Birthday and Façade numbers are incompatible, as with a 2 Birthday who has a 5 Facade or a 5 Birthday with a 2 Facade.

The Birthday will tell far more about an individual than the Façade any day. I analyze the Birthday as a single sum digit and if there are two numbers, I analyze each of them separately to bring out the subtle tones of the individuals personality. A double-digit Birthday number's positive characteristics increase with their compatibility.

I call the total of the birthdate (month, day, and year) the Façade because it is a minor indicator of how someone initially comes across to others. At best, the Façade is your outer self. The traits of the Birthday and Pinnacles reinforce or lessen the Façade. When the Façade is the same as the day of birth, or at least one of the Pinnacles, "What you see is what you get." However, the Façade never affects the numerological chart or a person's life. Those who call the Façade the birth path or destiny number say that this single number tells all about a person's personality, life and destiny. A single number in a person's numerological chart will tell you something about him, but none alone will tell you everything. I look at the composite effect of the entire numerological chart. This Façade number sometimes can be the cause of attracting the wrong people into your life, whether you keep them there depends on the influences in your chart and what you have learned from your experiences with the wrong types. The Façade also might make you seem to be something other than what you truly are. Below is a list of the sometimes-deceptive traits that come with each Façade. This Façade number always will be influenced by the day of birth number and the Pinnacles. As stated before, when the Façade number matches the Birthday number, "what you see is what you get."

1-independent, perhaps aloof

2-susceptible, an easy target, could attract needy types, users and controllers

3-friendly, people oriented

4-mysterious, difficult to see through

5-salesman, public relations like personality, people person

6-people person, attracts users and needy types, a good shield for deceivers

7-mysterious, not easy to get to know

8-take charge type, commanding, might attract control freaks

9-mature, very much in charge, a wise man or wise woman

The Birthday Number

I see the Birthday as the real you, your most intrinsic nature, and is the true measure of someone's personality and inherent nature. It is your personality, much of your character and, in some cases, it tells something about your appearance. I use the Birthday number in the same manner that many astrologers view the Ascendant or Rising sign. The day of birth indicates a strong or important part of your astrological chart, for example, your Ascendant or your Moon sign. However, the Pinnacles influence the Birthday, and the day of birth influences the Pinnacles. Knowing a person's month and day of birth alone will tell you quite a bit about him.

Chapter 3: What Is Numerology?

Throughout ancient history, numbers have held much spiritual significance. They were seen as something that had deep vibrational essence which contained magical messages. If we go into Mathematics deeper we can learn that the whole universe could be mapped out by the use of numbers and specific equations. So, if the whole of existence can be expressed by numbers then the power they hold over our lives must be almost limitless.

The philosophy of Numerology, goes way back, but we have no specific time of when it was first founded. It is one of the first recorded methods of metaphysical communicating, predicting and reading. The first recorded uses go as far back as ancient Egypt, which makes numerology thousands of years old. That is an awfully long time and there is no wonder that this art form is becoming popular once again.

Aside from the ancient Egyptians, there are strong sources connecting its use to ancient China, Japan, Rome and Greece. These were some of the most civilized cultures of their time, so it is of no real surprise that they were able to gain the universal significance of numbers. The fact that this art was discovered in various places around the world, places which had no real connection, strengthens the belief that Numerology is something really special as it managed to cross all cultural and distance bounds. Perhaps the philosophers who were accessing its effectiveness were all tuned into something much higher. A superior intelligence of some form, if this was the case than Numerology must have also come from a superior place. From the Gods, from the Universe or some cosmic divinity which we don't really know much about.

The modern form of Numerology we see today, is credited to the famous Greek philosopher Pythagoras, who also played a huge part in the development of modern day mathematics.

He would become a teacher and his specialities were in Maths, Music and Astronomy. His interest in Maths and Astronomy lead him to form a connection between the two and so he started exploring different uses for numbers. Until eventually he started to believe that the entire universe could be mapped out and expressed with numbers.

Pythagoras didn't invent Numerology but he is responsible for taking it to a new level which is how we now understand its use today. For this reason, he is often referred to as the 'Father of Numerology'. In modern times a lady by the name of Dr. Julia Stenton was responsible for increasing awareness of Numerology. There have been various schools of numerology created with their own techniques, but the meaning behind each number has always stayed the same.

There exist three main forms of Numerology - Chaldean, Kabbalic and Pythagorean. Kabbalic numerology comes from the Hebrew culture, whereas the Chaldean system was born from Mesopotamia (Greek) culture and is strongly related to Astrology since they both originated from the same place. All three methods can be used together to give a more comprehensive reading. However, it is generally advised to stick to one system. The teachings of this book are based on the Pythagorean teachings, which is the most popular form in the west.

From these early teachings, we can learn that numbers held a high degree of spiritual significance and that each number had a certain power. This is expressed not only by their symbols but also by each numbers connection to universal laws. Numbers are connected to all things. Everything in our world can be broken down into an equation which signifies the very thing of interest.

The Meaning of Each Number (0-9)

As we all know, there exists only ten different individual numbers. From these ten however, we can create an infinite combination of outcomes and figures. In this chapter, we look at the spiritual significance of each of these ten numbers. Many of us are often drawn to a certain number for no apparent reasons. Children often have a favourite number. Now you can find out the meanings of them all and see any reasons you may have favoured any one number in particular.

On the other hand, we may look at the following meanings and decided to choose a new favoured number. Perhaps the meaning of this new number resonates with us more deeply than the one we were previously keen on.

Number 1

The number 1 is well-known for being at the top. Athletes and all sport teams strive for the top spot. In fact, most of our society is based on being number 1. The best. But what does this special number actually represent?

This number is seen as a strong symbol of will, individuality, positivity and self-empowerment. It is strongly related to new beginnings and exploring of the self. This means, knowing the power that we each hold within ourselves while aligning with our higher self. It is also recognized as a masculine number since it forms the shape of an arrow. This signifies focusing our energy outwards.

Number 2

If we compare number 2 to number 1, then it probably isn't seen as favourably. As the saying goes 'second place is the first loser'. With this type of belief most people tend to think of the number 2 in a negative way. But, we should keep an open mind and learn the truth of what this number actually means.

This number is in fact very different from the number 1. This number is more about balance, kindness and equality. The Chinese Yin Yang symbol represents the number 2 perfectly as it shows the balance between male and female. It means working in harmony with others, communicating and co-operating in order to find the perfect solution. Partnership and union are other words which help give the number two its identity.

Number 3

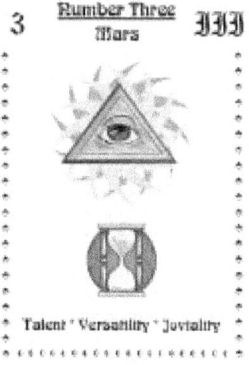

This number is related to intuition, magic and symbolizes all the divine parts of the body-mind-spirit coming together. It shows authentic creativity, natural expression and versatility. It is also strongly related to time, since three-dimensional time exists as past, present and future. The energy of this number uses magic to activate positive thoughts to create positive opportunities in the future. Which promotes our ability to succeed.

Number 4

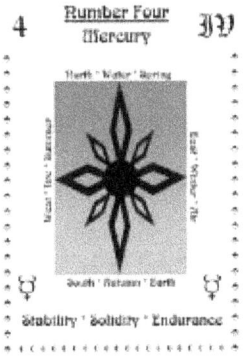

The number 4 symbolizes stability in this physical world. It links the mind, body and spirit to the world. It keeps us grounded and in control through organization and structure. Take for example, the four seasons - Spring, Summer, Autumn and Winter. All four work together in harmony to create the perfect environment for life to thrive on Earth. It also stands for safety, solidity, security and calmness. If we experience seeing this number often it may mean we need to center ourselves and get back to feeling grounded. Use this number to build a strong foundation.

Number 5

This is the strongest number related to manifestation. It represents the five elements of life - Fire, Earth, Air, Water and Ether. All five parts are all that is needed in order to manifest anything. It also relates to adventure, travel and expansion which all represent freedom. The freedom to live our dreams and go after whatever resides in our heart. If this number constantly pops up in your life get ready for action, like a new business venture, a relationship or a trip. It does also carry with it change, unpredictability and instability.

Number 6

This number symbolizes guidance and 'seeing' through our own inner wisdom. If we follow this path all the way, it will inevitably lead to enlightenment. It also represents harmony, love and truth. It gives us the confidence to believe that events are unfolding in the best way possible way for everyone involved.

Finally, it tells us to use our abilities of visualization and imagination so we can create what we desire.

Number 7

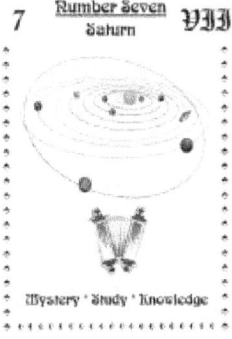

This number is probably one of the more popular numbers since it symbolizes luck, for this reason people are naturally drawn toward it. The number 7 is strongly related to the number 3, since they are both connected to magic. Seven allows us to receive divine vibrations and is a strong spiritual number which is charged with the energy of luck and synchronicity, this is where the term 'Lucky number 7' comes from. It promotes opening of the chakras and improves our natural intuitiveness. If this is a strong number for us, we will be guided by our feelings and be able to open up to receive divine wisdom. This number is ruled by Saturn and promotes manifestation through conscious thought and awareness.

Number 8

The number 8 symbolizes wealth, abundance and prosperity. The Universe provides unlimited abundance to those who are attuned to its power. It allows the flow of money to us since it shows continuation, cycles and repetition. These attributes are clearly shown in the symbolism of the number just as success is often the result of repetition and determination. Also, businesses rely on 'cycles' to bring back finance to them. Number 8 also teaches us self-empowerment through living in harmony with the rest of the world.

Number 9

The number 9 brings us to the height of all numbers and for this reason it relates to 'Cosmic consciousness'. It is through this realization we can open up to the higher self. This number means completion, accomplishment and satisfaction, while allowing one to see from a higher spiritual perspective and see the divine play of life. Once we are ready to learn what our deepest purpose is, the number 9 will show us. Finally, it teaches us look within for our inner attributes and how to use them to serve the world and to make a positive difference.

Number 0

This number is quite interesting because in of itself, it doesn't have any value.

But when it is added to other numbers if can multiply their value infinitely. The main principle behind the number zero is pure potentiality (Deepak Chopra). This is the starting point for all over numbers. The shape of the number zero symbolizes an egg, a womb or a seed, which are all new beginnings. It's circular shape also shows eternity and never ending evolution. The 0 is where all creative potential comes from. Paradoxically, it stands for nothingness and oneness (everything). Just as the number 1 is masculine the zero is feminine, open. If we are trying to remain in the moment, focusing on the meaning of zero is recommended. The idea that it symbolizes everything and nothing all at once, perplexes us into the present moment.

The meanings of each number shown here are a glimpse of their true significance and power. We should allow our inner knowing to be activated when learning and discovering what each number means to us.

Although the essential numbers are covered I also felt it was interesting to look at other popular numbers, most notably the number 13 and the number 10. These two numbers have a strong meaning for most people.

Number 10

This is the first number following the essential numbers (0-9) and is seen as the number of destiny. When the code of the universe is broken down, it is in a code of what's called binary numbers, which are all 1's and 0's. This means that these are the numbers which hold the information for creation. For that reason, the number 10 tells us that our destiny is written in the stars in this binary code. It is as though all your life possibilities can be calculated using this code to create your experience. The trick is to learn how to decipher the code and work out exactly what is going on and where we are headed. As we begin to get in-tune with our truth and destiny, we start to work with the Universes natural codes and laws, which then guide us to achieve whatever desire.

Number 13

This is another number I felt deserved a mention since it is deemed to be unlucky and has a lot of negativity attached to it. This well-known number represents rebellion and upheaval. But not always in a negative sense, as revolts can also make way for something new and positive. This number holds power which can be used selfishly that can then cause destruction to the self and others. Alternatively, its power can be harnessed to create good. This number is also related to problems in life. But with perseverance they can be handled and then the power of the number can be used to help propel us forward.

One of the reasons it may be seen as unlucky is because of its link to Satan. In the Bible 'the dragon' is seen to represent Satan and is found 13 times in the biblical text Revelation.

Hopefully, this chapter gives a greater understanding behind the meaning of each number and you may find some aspects of each number resonate with you.

Chapter 4: Destiny Number

The purpose, goal and direction of your life.

Write down your name in full, and under each letter write down its numerological value. Add these numbers together and reduce the calculation until you have either a master number or a single digit.

Use your full name as given at birth even if that isn't the name you're now known by. Your original name acts as a blueprint for your life. It defines the tools and talents you were born with and the types of people and experiences you're likely to attract. Your destiny number shows potential and qualities you can cultivate. The challenges of this number may not always be easy, but it's your goal and life's purpose. While your life path number describes what you **are**, your destony number describes what you must **do**.

You can also analyse any changed or shortened name you use or have used. This number will be more relevant to you at the time of your life you most often used that version of your name. And if you were adopted, you may have been given a different name to your birth name. That acts as an amendment to your original blueprint and there may sometimes be friction between the two names. The same applies to any other change of name. If you work under a professional name, the destiny number for that name will apply to your life in that environment.

You seek to grow by gaining greater independence and establishing yourself as a leader. You are good at organising and have a creative approach to problem solving along with being capable of initiating action. Although you're not so good with details, you know how to make things happen. You have a good mind and prefer to act on your own. You are ambitious, determined, confident and self-reliant with the courage of your convictions. You hate to be stuck in a routine. Beware of being self-centred and bossy.

You seek to grow by gaining an understanding of people and the world around you. You work well with others and are a natural mediator. Capable of leading by example, you can make an excellent teacher. Functioning best in a partnership or as part of a group, you don't seek acclaim and can be modest about your achievements. You are cooperative and considerate, able to handle people well and you pay close attention to detail. Sometimes, you are a dreamer rather than a doer and you can be impractical. Beware of being over sensitive.

You seek to grow by developing your creativity. Your life is likely to involve the use of words, for example, as a writer, actor or teacher. You can sell yourself or any product. You are optimistic and enthusiastic. As you're friendly and sociable, people like you because you're charming and a good conversationalist. Beware of being superficial too easy-going and scattering your energy.

You seek to grow by establishing order. You have good organisational skills with a practical, down to earth approach. Being willing to work long, hard hours and patience with detail allows you to become expert in fields like building and engineering. You are responsible and fulfil your obligations as well as being systematic and orderly. You are also serious and sincere, honest and faithful. When it comes to friends, you have high standards, and spend time with those with high moral values. Beware of being stubborn, dogmatic or prejudiced.

You seek to grow by bringing forth change. You are likely to be multi-talented and versatile, capable of doing many things well. Freedom is important to you, and you are good at presenting ideas and knowing how to approach people to get what you want. You are clever, analytical and a quick thinker. At times you are restless and impatient. Beware of being rebellious for the sake of being rebellious and scattering your energy.

You seek to grow by being helpful and considerate. Highly responsible, you are conscientious, and capable of rectifying any inharmonious situation. You are a loving, friendly, appreciative person with a depth of understanding. You are naturally inclined towards being helpful and may end up working in a caring role. Domestic activities appeal to you and openness and honesty part of your approach to all relationships. Beware of being too self-righteous and over worrying.

You seek to grow by increasing your knowledge. You seek to develop your mind in order to search out the truth. Little escapes your observation and deep understanding. It is likely that you value solitude. Your intention is to become an authority on whatever you focus on, and you like to work alone in your own way, with a logical and rational approach. At times, you have problems with dealing with emotional situations. Beware of being overly critical and intolerant and too perfectionist.

You seek to grow by achieving material success and raising your status. Ambitious and goal oriented, you can plan, initiate, and complete projects. Highly organised, you could establish or operate a business with great efficiency. You will receive material rewards for your efforts, and have good judgment when it comes to money. You are also a good judge of character. Highly confident, you can be impatient with lesser mortals and slow progress. You may follow your ambitions to the detriment of the other important factors in your life. Beware of being intolerant.

You seek to grow by being compassionate towards others. Sensitive towards the needs of others, you have the potential to inspire. You have creative ability and a strong sense of imagination. Friendships and love are extremely important to you. When following your ambitions, you remain sympathetic and tolerant towards others and are broad-minded. At times you may be aloof and uninvolved, concerned more with humanistic interests than individuals. Beware of being selfish.

You seek to grow by inspiring others and teaching what you know. You can be inspirational and lead by example. Your intuition is strong and you possess a keen mind.keywords You work with ideals and have a strong sense of intuition. More of a dreamer than a doer, you are sometimes impractical. Your thinking is long term, and can be disappointed by the short-sighted views of those around you. Beware of being over sensitive.

You seek to grow by resolving problems with new approaches. You will be extremely capable at whatever you choose to do in life. You are especially equipped to handle large-scale undertakings. You have unorthodox approaches to problem solving. As a strong leader, you aren't afraid to go in new directions. You are an idealist, with the material skills to build and develop for the good of all. Your inner strength is clearly visible, and if developed, this strength will possess the charisma to attract a following. Beware of being eccentric, domineering and overbearing.

You seek to grow by uncovering and supplying what people truly need. Deeply compassionate, you can fulfil the needs of those around you and you are capable of intuitive insight into their needs. You may have to sacrifice what you want for the benefit of others. Beware of becoming a martyr.

Chapter 5: The Spiritual Angle To Numerology

Are you thinking of religion here? Well, do not – because numerology looks at that mystical aspect of numbers that relates to you as a person. That is the spiritual angle we are referring to here – nothing to do with creeds or denominations. There is a divine manner in which your characteristics are tied to your number and it goes beyond our understanding. It is a relationship that neither you nor anyone else can dismantle. You have the opportunity, though, to tune your activities to be in sync with your life path. You also have the opportunity to downplay those attributes that make your relationship with other people a bit rough.

Femininity and Masculinity of Numbers

And did you know there are personal attributes that are generally accepted as being feminine while others are basically masculine? Consequently, there are some Life Path numbers that denote femininity, others masculinity, and still others that have got an aspect of both. But you need to understand that this whole clarification has nothing to do with whether you were born female or male.

Here is what your Life Path numbers mean:

Number One (1)

This number is symbolized by the sun. Of course, you know the sun is a strong natural source of energy; pure energy, we might add, as it comes straight from the source and reaches you unadulterated. It also does not leave any by-products along the way.

Now, if you are a One, you have no problem with energy. You are actually physically and mentally energetic. In addition to your great energy is the fact that you have strong will power. You also have a positive outlook to life.

When it comes to the aspect of femininity and masculinity, number ones are generally masculine. They take up the leadership role in a natural way; and they are not afraid also to take a lone position with firmness. They are usually organized and also ambitious.

Wow! Great qualities, those ones are... But then, there is the other side of the coin. Do you realize that taking on a leadership role as a matter of fact and helping the group succeed with apparent ease does not always augur well for some people? Some of the people present may have had something positive to contribute but are slow in expressing their sentiments. The sheer fact that they were not entirely empty of ideas makes them feel unfairly overshadowed; something that has potential of breeding contempt towards you.

This is where knowledge of numerology becomes handy. Once you realize you are a Number One, you can put yourself in check so that you consciously slow down to give others an opportunity to come out and shine.

Number Two (2)

This number is feminine and is symbolized by the moon. When you are a two, you are one of those people that are able to appreciate both sides of an argument. You approach issues in a peaceful way and choose to resolve conflicts in a quiet manner. Let us say, you are simply a diplomat. In this respect, you are right the opposite of Number One.

You are also known for your kindness. You like to keep things simple while embracing the truth. But is there a downside to Number 2?

Oh yes. The world is not known for its fairness otherwise good people would always be rewarded in a commensurate manner. But in the case of Number 2s, some people tend to see them as being cowardly; subservient; or just shy. As such, if you are one, you may need to be alert not to be misused by the extroverts.

Number Three (3)

Have you heard of the Trinity? Something to do with the Christian God, Son and the Holy Spirit – Three-in-One Holy entity? Now in numerology, that is what is equated to Number Three. Also Mars is used symbolically for the 3s. Number 3s are taken to be harmonious and great at mediation. Number 3s are also very active, sociable, versatile and with very good communication skills. Their characteristics fall under the masculine.

Well, these are very admirable traits. Any downside…? Sure – sometimes they come across as superficial.

Number Four (4)

Fours fall under the feminine arm. They are calm and display a sense of endurance. They give a sense of homeliness and are naturally grounded. They are symbolized by four dimensions, seasons, directions, sides of a cube and so on. 4s are stable and assured of themselves; and they are, undoubtedly, hard working. On the overall, they make very good employees. So far so good; but do they have weaknesses?

They sure do. But they are weaknesses they can work on once they are aware of them by appreciating numerology; example being that they are so set on achieving their goals that they fail to take time to savor the niceties of life. For that reason, they are usually indifferent and dull.

Number Five (5)

See this masculine number as being represented by the Star because of the star's five pointers; and the set of four limbs plus your head. It is also symbolized by the planet Jupiter.

As for character, 5s are adventurous and fun-loving. They also have a great sense of humor and are fun to be with. They think and act fast and hence are able to handle unexpected challenges with relative ease. Above that, they cherish their freedom.

But theirs, like all other Life Path numbers, are not entirely rosy. They often take too much risk, something that can sometimes be unsettling and destabilizing. They are also quick-tempered and unpredictable.

Number Six (6)

Do you not love people who are compassionate and quick to forgive? Well, those are the sixes. They are the ones to go for when there is a delicate matter that needs to be handled with high level of diplomacy. Six is feminine; and is influenced by Venus. Sixes have the natural motherly instincts – warm; nurturing; giving; and also a sense of security. They are responsible and supportive; and they strive to find solutions to problems.

The downside…? Well, sixes sometimes come across as know-it-alls; people who are prone to interfering with other people's business.

Number Seven (7)

While nobody is going superstitious here, it is important to mention that there is something magical about the sevens; including having some psychic abilities. They are said to be influenced by Saturn and they are masculine. They are introspective and reflective; and tend to be drawn towards the mystic. Something that could make you envy these people is the way they care less about material things yet they seem to get money with relative ease. They are also highly intellectual.

When it comes to how they behave, they are practically loners who, nevertheless, work very well without the need to be supervised. In contrast to other people who go out seeking company when they find themselves alone, the sevens choose to drift into dreamland and do not even lavish themselves with rest or sleep.

So what is it that makes others uncomfortable about the sevens? Well, they come across as very distant to others, and sometimes even cold. They are also seen as anti-social.

Number Eight (8)

Eights are influenced greatly by Uranus; and they happen to be clearly feminine. They are evidently very hard working and family oriented. And, do you like wealth? Well, eights are crazy about wealth accumulation. They are tough and strive to accomplish tasks in order to be successful. They do exemplary well in business.

But you may not always like the eights; reason being that the extreme focus they have on success often pushes them to ruthlessness. They are also extremely impatient.

Number Nine (9)

The Nines are masculine and are high achievers too. They also have drive and high ideals; brilliant ideas; and they are also broad in outlook. They think of how they can solve issues at global level. They are highly energetic and are always seeking ways of improving projects. They are inventive and are geared towards influencing matters. They have an extremely creative knack that makes them enjoy traveling to far off places.

Even as they strive to achieve, they are quick to forget the past accomplishments as they look out for other challenges. The adverse effect of that attribute is that they are easy to let go of relationships when they feel like they have outlived their usefulness. They also appear to be egocentric.

Number Eleven (11)

The Elevens have both feminine and masculine attributes. They are intuitive; sensible; and very practical. Here is the beauty of the Elevens: They carry some great qualities from the Ones – owing to their composition of 1 and 1; and they also carry some great qualities of the Twos – simply because 1+1 reduces to 2. So with the masculinity of One and the femininity of Two, the Elevens are greatly balanced.

Number Twenty-Two (22)

This one is feminine, which should not surprise you considering that it could reduce to 4 – 2 plus 2; and we have seen that 4 is actually feminine. In numerology, Twenty-Two is symbolized by the Tree of Life. The Twenty-twos have many great qualities from Number 2.

There is plenty more you could learn about the significance of various numbers in numerology, but suffice it to say that understanding numerology is like having a torch to see your way ahead; you cannot stumble too much.

Chapter 6: Meaning Of Birth Date Numbers

Your birth date has an added influence to your life Path. It's like a modifier to your life path. Interest is on the exact day you were born. You brought some inborn traits into this life, which affects your Life Path. Let's now look deeper into the births occurring on different days of any month.

1st day

This indicates that you have extra leadership qualities and executive ability than indicated in your life path. Being born on any month's first day portrays a higher will power, self-confidence, and creativity due to number 1 energy. However, you may lower your attention to details, and brush lightly over matters. You also suppress your sensitivity.

2nd day

This day indicates excess emotions, friendliness, intuition, and sensitivity. You are nervous in front of many people, warmhearted, more prone to depression and anxiety, moody, and have a hard time bouncing back after setbacks.

3rd day

You have extra vitality. This 3 energy enables you to bounce back quickly after any setback. You are also impatient and sometimes portray an easygoing and carefree attitude. You have great public address skills and a good impressionist. Therefore, you excel in speaking, writing, and singing. You tend to energetic and imaginative but tend to be a busy body often biting more than you can chew, affectionate but sensitive and experience many life's ups and downs.

4th day

This day indicates you are a better organizer and manager and more responsible and self-disciplined than shown on your Life Path. You are also honest, sincere, practical, rational, hardworking and detail conscious. If this number appears more than once in your reading, its energies can repress emotions and increase stubbornness.

5th day

Being born on this day shows you enjoy company and work well with others. You are flexible, creative, adaptable, clever, analytical, and talented and express ideas well. You like change and travel, are impatient and bored with routine but avoid responsibilities,

6th day

If born on this day, you are more helpful, honest, caring, responsible, understanding and concerned with others than your life path indicates.

7th day

Being born on this day portrays that you are a perfectionist and individualistic. You provide excellent mental analysis and reasoning. You are more psychic and sensitive, and intuitive. You are also a lone worker and dislike being bossed around. You also tend to be self-centered and stubborn.

8th day

Born on this day indicates you are an excellent businessperson, planner, salesperson, decision maker and have higher personal judgment. This means that you should be your own boss, since you are controlling and handle money well. You make time for important matters and will succeed materially beyond your wildest dreams.

9th day

Being born on this day indicates you are more idealistic and humanitarian. You are tolerant, broadminded, and generous, more sympathetic and compassionate than your core number shows. You can also be overgenerous.

10th day

Being born on this day portrays you are energetic and independent, are a good manager and executive than your Life Path indicates. In addition, you have all the other number 1 energies and qualities.

11th day

Being born on this day indicates you are a dreamer and an idealist, which makes you more persuasive, spiritual and intuitive, sensitive and temperamental. You are also highly analytical hence you are good in business and overly creative which makes you more of a dreamer than a doer.

12th day

You are born with triple energies, which highly increase your vitality in life. In addition, you have all the qualities associated with being born on the 3rd day.

13th day

Being born on the 13th makes you a better manager and organizer but very dominating. You may also be more self-disciplined and responsible than your Life

Path suggests. This 4 energy makes you honest, serious and hardworking if the number 4 appears elsewhere in your reading. You also tend to repress emotions and feelings and have all the other qualities associated with fourth day.

14th day

Born on the 14th day means you have the 5 energy, enjoy company and work well with others. You are talented and versatile with good presentation and organization skills. You also like to travel and make changes. You tend to avoid issues and responsibilities and have all the other qualities of those born on the 5th day

15th day

Being born on this day means you are more attached to family, home and domestic affairs. The 1 and 5 totaling to 6, gives you the energy that makes you an excellent teacher or parent, very capable and responsible. You are harmonious, a mediator and learn by observing. You don't like instructions and are more artist and talented than you think and very generous but stubborn.

16th day

Being born on the 16th day adds to your sense of loneliness and preference to work alone. You are inflexible and independent while you enjoy to rest and to meditate. You are stubborn but introspective and therefore you have problems maintaining outside relationships and would rather be at home with family. You are more religious, spiritual, scientific, and technical and like to explore on untouched territories. You have inborn intuition but mostly act logically and use a responsible rational approach to issues. You repress your emotions so don't give or get that much desired affection.

17th day

Being born on the 17th day, increases your financial fortune because this date is considered to have extra good business sense and interest. You can be very ethical and honest but shrewd and prosperous in business world and commercial enterprise. You have excellent managerial, organizational, and administrative skills hence in a position to take on huge projects with big budgets at ease. You are also ambitious and focused though you don't finish projects you start in most cases. You repress your emotions so you don't give or get that much desired affection.

18th day

Being born on this date suggests that you work well in groups but similarly prefer to keep a personal identity. Your approach to business matters is a humanistic or philanthropic. You are an excellent decision maker, organizer, and administrator. You are also tolerant, broad-minded, generous, compassionate, inspiring, and imaginative. You express a few emotions but suppress most and express yourself dramatically. Give without expecting to be given back.

19th day

Being born on this day provides your life path with extra independence and energy. However, you have to overcome huge obstacles before you attain total independence. The number 1 energy improves on your leadership qualities and executive ability than that indicated on your life path. You also have increased self-confidence, will power and creativity but also selfish, lack attention to details so brush lightly over issues, repress your sensitivity, dominating, dislike advice and prefer to learn through experience and more irritable and anxious than suggested by your life path. You feel lonely even in marriage because 19/1 is a loner number.

20th day

Being born on this day increases your sensitivity, emotions, and intuition on your reading. The 2 energy makes you social and friendly but nervous in large groups. You are warm hearted and emotional and always in search of affection. Being too emotional makes you vulnerable to depression, moodiness, anxiety, and mental confusion. Depression limits your ability to come back to reality. You also tend to be overly affectionate.

21st day

Being born on such a day triples your energy hence increases on your vitality. The 3 energy allows you to recover from physical and mental setbacks fast. Impatient and sometimes portray an easy going and carefree attitude. Have great public address skills and a good impressionist. You excel in speaking, writing and singing, are energetic and imaginative but often tend to be a busy body biting more than you can chew. You are also affectionate but sensitive. You experience many ups and downs in life.

22nd day

Your approaches are sometimes unconventional. You can take over and handle huge tasks and even put extra effort to complete them. You also tend to be stubborn and repress your feelings especially in your earlier years. You have great charisma and inner strength, idealistic and work towards a greater good. You are also a good organizer though lack attention to detail. You are very mindful and intuitive but also nervous.

23rd day

Being born on this day gives you the 5 energy. You enjoy working with others, are versatile, talented and present ideas perfectly. You like change and travel, impatient and bored with routine. You are social, good at making friends and a perfect travel partner but avoid responsibilities.

24th day

Being born on this day increase on your responsibility and humanitarian capacity than your life path indicates. You become more a peacemaker and mediator during conflict, and devoted to family whom you highly protect. You have increased emotions and sensitivity and you enjoy both giving and receiving affection.

25th day

Being born on this day gives you the 7 energy which transforms your life path by adding on your interest towards scientific, technical and complex knowledge. You tend to become a perfectionist, are too attentive to detail, intuitive, rational, responsible, inventive, and have unique approaches and solutions to problems. You have deep feelings but you suppress them, tend to be more private, introspective and even more rigid. In any relationship, you are very reserved and cautious.

26th day

Being born on this day gives you the 8 energy which changes your life path by improving on your business skills and success. The combination of 2 and 6 energies enable you to work well with others. An improvement is made on your managerial, organizational, and administrative abilities. You are good at handling money and efficient, energetic and ambitious while cooperative and adaptable. You are also reliable, responsible, diplomatic, sociable and persuasive. You can combine well attention to detail and skimming through matters and are very good at finishing what you start. You also tend to be realistic, practical and seeker of material satisfaction.

27th day

The 9 energy on this day increases on your selflessness and humanitarianism than indicated on your life path. You can definitely work well with others, but require some alone time to rest and meditate. Irrespective of your life path number, you are more humanistic and charitable. You are also tolerant, broadminded, cooperative, very generous, persuasive, very sensitive to others' feelings and needs and give more than you receive.

28th day

This day gives you extra energy, which adds independence and vitality to your Life Path. Number 1 energy increase your executive skill and leadership potentials than indicated on your life path. Being born on 28th makes you acquire greater creativity, will power and self-confidence. Unlike those born on the 1st day, this day enhances your ability to start and finish tasks. You can skim through issues but also pay attention to details. You tend to be sensitive but repress it. You are also dominating.

29th day

The 29th day increases your creativity and imagination but makes you less comfortable in business. You are very mindful, sensitive, analytical, and intuitive. The 29 is reduced to 11, which is a master number therefore makes you often nervous. You tend to be a dreamer than a doer but cope well with others.

30th day

Being born on this day shows that self-expression is an important factor in your happiness. You use words to express yourself in a clear and understandable manner and excel in areas requiring skill with words. You give very dramatic presentations, which makes you a natural mimic or a potential actor. You can be a good writer or storyteller due to your deep imagination. You are also opinionated and think you are always right and sometimes scatter your energies hence you don't complete tasks well. You are a very creative and talented artist.

31st day

Being born on this day you are a great manager and organizer, are energetic and dependable, which makes you successful in business. You are sincere, patient and determined to accomplish a lot in life. Approach issues creatively but often stubborn. You may also be sensitive but repress emotions. You pay great attention to detail and accurate but sometimes scatter energies and often practical with little imagination. You don't enjoy living alone and enjoy travel. Its good you marry early for responsibility will increase on your stability.

Chapter 7: What Your Expression Number Says About You

Do you recall the expression number being mentioned as one of your core numbers? It brings out your personality so that you can even tell where in society you fit best. Actually, your expression number tells you who you really are inherently. As such, you can adapt to varying environments accordingly to make the best out of life.

How to Establish Your Expression Number

What you need to know at this juncture is that you derive your expression number from your full name – not your first name or middle name alone, but your entire name.

Why do you think that is the case?

The reality is that a lot of thinking normally goes into picking your name. And so the energies transmitted during that time of selecting your name have a lot to do with whom you are.

Simple calculations to get your expression number

Let us suppose you have the conventional three names: your first name, your middle name as well as your surname. The systematic way of getting your expression number is to first add up the numbers that correspond to the letters of each individual name.

Question – how do you tell which number corresponds to what letter?

In numerology, you continue to use the single digit master numbers. In our case here, you will be able to tell where each of the letters of your name falls using the simple tabulation below. And then you can proceed with your additions till you get your ultimate single digit.

One	Two	Three	Four	Five	Six	Seven	Eight	Nine

A	B	C	D	E	F	G	H	I
J	K	L	M	N	O	P	Q	R
S	T	U	V	W	X	Y	Z	

Example

Tom Ike Smith

Tom = 2+6+4 = 12

Ike = 9+2+5 = 16

Smith = 1+4+9+2+8 = 24

Since each of those names has produced a double digit, you need to do some further addition that will leave each of them with a single digit.

12 = 1+2 = 3

16 = 1+6 = 7

24 = 2+4 = 6

Great! Now, remembering that you just need a single digit to be able to read what your life holds for you, it is important that you add up those single digits resulting from your individual names.

3+7+6 = 16

And any double digit has to be reduced to one digit. Therefore:

1+6 = 7

And you straightaway know that Tom Ike Smith has **seven** as his expression number.

Meanings of Expression Numbers

Number 1

Number ones are so independent that they do not mind undertaking projects all on their own. They have natural leadership abilities. However, with their drive, they often alienate people they would have loved to take along on their journey to success, including family and friends.

Number 2

Number two people are highly intuitive, friendly and also sensitive. They are open-minded and very supportive. Often others take the limelight during times of success, without them realizing that the number two was actually the reason the success came about.

The flipside is that the degree of sensitivity that these people have can often be a cause for discouragement especially when others speak negatively about them.

Number Three

People in this category are outgoing, expressive and vivacious. Whereas they are social, they still have a tendency of leaving others out as they get involved in activities that help them utilize their energy. At the same time, they lack the necessary focus to see issues matters to their logical conclusion.

Number Four

Here is where you find the organized lot. Even when they deviate from their most common professions of accountancy, bookkeeping, law, and so on, they still take order with them in those other fields that attract them like music or even art.

The downside is that they can be too stubborn and moralistic. In effect they are unable to adjust as circumstances change, sometimes even appearing to be short of compassion.

Number Five

Number five people are full of excitement and enthusiasm and people love them for it. It rejuvenates their spirits. Their love for freedom leads them to adventure even within their careers.

Nevertheless, these people sometimes go overboard and take too much risk in their quest for adventure.

Number Six

Number six people are selfless. They tend to support other people at the cost of their own ambitions and goals. They are creative, caring and also trustworthy.

Number Seven

Number seven people are deep thinkers who seek to find answers to things that appear complex or mystical. They have a great urge to be furnished with knowledge and to capture the truth. They are, for instance, comfortable delving into scientific matters and issues of philosophy.

However, these people have a tendency to keep away from the social scene coming across as being aloof.

Number Eight

These are highly driven people with great leadership qualities. They also have the ability to judge people's character with reasonable precision. The downside is that sometimes they focus so much on their goals that they become oblivious of the feelings of other people. What is required of people with expression number eight is a fair balance between their push for success and a bit of spirituality.

Number Nine

Here lies the idealists; people who derive the greatest pleasure from seeing the world improve in all ways possible. These are people with no prejudices and often fail to judge people correctly. Despite their loving and caring nature, people with expression number nine are hardly able to express their sincere feelings. However, their demeanor still attracts people to them.

Double Digit Master Numbers

When it comes to getting information from expression numbers, you are not expected to reduce the double digit master numbers to a single digit. There is information for them as they stand.

Number Eleven

You are quite emotional with a high energy surge and you have a great presence that you are not conscious about. In fact, that energy flow, some of which comes from deep in your unconscious, can get you into emotional instability if you do not deliberately put it under check.

Although you have the ability to balance your energies by looking at issues from a human perspective rather than spiritual, you often find yourself being too dependent on relationships; something that can take you on an emotional roller coaster.

Number Twenty-two

Number twenty-two people have great potential. They have a broad perspective of the world that is not inhibited by racial or such other differences. They dream of utilizing their potential to make a positive mark in the world. However, there is another aspect of them that pulls them to slow down on risk taking. Though they often listen to that inner voice and often let chances pass, they still end up succeeding within their own set limits.

Chapter 8: Understanding Numbers And Digits

SINGLE-DIGIT NUMBERS

Each of the first single digit numbers from 1 to 9 is associated with an array of traits and qualities that make it unique and recognizable. In numerology, each number, just like any human being, is a character. You need to learn about the traits of each single digit as if it were a person in order to comprehend how they affect us according to where they are located in the chart. The aim is to get beyond a number being all about positive and negative traits and instead make it come alive and sense how it plays off of other digits and numbers. If you feel like some numbers have been given exaggerative descriptions, you might want to think of the kinds of individuals we have – some being more extreme than others, and others even seeming to portray beyond-human characteristics.

One (1)

Positive traits

1s are independent and individualistic with drive and a sense of leadership. They are self-starters and originators, rebellious in a good way, courageous, strong-willed, progressive, focused and masculine.

Negative traits

1s can be undisciplined, weak, selfish, stubborn, dominating, overly assertive, impulsive and willful – characteristics common with egoistic and independent people.

Two (2) – The all knowing

Positive traits

Caring, compassionate, considerate and sensitive to other people's needs and problems. They believe in diplomacy - something they are good at - are loving, peacemakers/mediators, patient and studious. They may express intuitiveness and a lot of feminine or musical qualities.

Negative traits

2s tend to be too much into other people's issues, even when their help is not needed. They can be a little bit careless with the truth, are shy and self-conscious and can get oversensitive when criticized with their faults.

Three (3) – Mr. Creativity

Positive traits

Possess artistic skills, and are imaginative and expressive communicators. They are optimistic, inspiring, dynamic, jovial, youthful, and let themselves enjoy life fully.

Negative traits

3s are self-centered, moody, leave projects unfinished, are intolerant and impatient, and happen to be exaggerative on simple issues.

Four (4) – salt of the earth

Positive traits

4s are pragmatic, stable, trustworthy, patriotic, focused, reliable/dependable, frugal, conscientious, methodical, precise, humble, hardworking and emotionally strong.

Negative traits

Pragmatism and stability associated with 4s comes at a price. People often find 4s boring. This can be greatly attributed to their low sense of imagination, empathy and emotions. They care less about their appearances, and this social awkwardness makes them seem, jealous, crude or vulgar.

Five (5) – a dynamic force

Positive traits

They are freedom-loving, energetic, daring, worldly and adventurous. They also tend to be witty and quick-thinking, courageous, sensual, social, curios, adaptable, flexible and versatile.

Negative traits

On the other side of the coin, 5s can be careless and irresponsible, self-indulgent, chaotic and unstable. They are likely to indulge themselves in drug and alcohol abuse as well as caring less about education.

Six (6) – the caretaker

Positive traits

6s are compassionate, sympathetic, self-sacrificing, protective, loving and responsible. They make good teachers and parents.

Negative traits

The protectiveness that makes 6s the parental figures they are also acts as a con to them in that they may become over-worrisome, paranoid, suspicious, emotionally unstable, anxious, jealous or cynical. They tend towards the conventional side.

Seven (7) – the seeker

Positive traits

Seven is widely known to be a lucky number, but that's not all it stands for. 7s are spiritual, knowledgeable, intelligent, focused, analytical, introspective, gracious, refined, serious, contemplative, intuitive, studious and display much inner wisdom.

Negative traits

7s can be unfriendly, sarcastic, distant, aloof, melancholic, socially awkward, cowardly, and can be backstabbers at their worst.

Eight (8) – power and balance

Positive traits

8s are authoritative and tend to value power and control, yet very balanced. They are business minded, realistic, successful and materially detached. They are good character judges, street-smart, capable and efficient, which most of the time lands them in leadership and managerial posts.

Negative traits

On the flip side, 8s can be greedy, bullish, violent, cruel and very insensitive. They can also be intolerant religious enthusiasts at their worst.

Nine (9) – global awareness

Positive traits

9s are self-sacrificing, helpful, compassionate, charitable, humanitarian, generous, cooperative and romantic.

Negative traits

They can be too proud, egocentric, cold, arrogant, sentimental, self-pitying, fickle, discontent and mentally unstable.

MASTER NUMBERS

Eleven (11) – most intuitive

Of all numbers, 11 is the most intuitive. 11s are basically dreamers. They portray illumination, impracticality, shyness, nervous energy, illumination and can also be a link to the subconscious. It has all aspects of the 2 energy such as possession of good leadership skills, being charismatic and being inspirational. It's a number with the ability to create dynamism and create inner conflict with its mere presence. It can however be turned inward to bring phobias and fears if not well focused on a goal beyond itself. It walks the edge between self-destruction and greatness. It's the psychic's number; not of logic but faith.

Twenty Two (22) – most powerful

22 is more powerful than any other number. It's commonly referred to as the Master Builder. It's potentially more successful than any other number and possesses the ability to turn into reality the most ambitious of dreams. Combined with the practicality that comes with the 4 energy, it has many inspirational insights present in 11. It portrays self-confidence, leadership, idealism, big ideas and great plans. Unfortunately, not all 22s are practical. Most of them waste their potential and sometimes the big ambitions can turn into serious internal pressures,

just like the 11. Generally, though, 22s serve the world in a more practical way.

Thirty Three (33) – most influential

Commonly referred to as the Master Teacher, 33 is the most influential number. It combines aspects in both the 11 and the 22, bringing the potential in them to another level. It does not focus on realizing personal goals but rather works in its power towards mankind's spiritual uplifting. Its unmatched level of devotion particularly makes it quite impressive. This is exhibited in its determination to seek wisdom and sufficient understanding on subjects before preaching to other people. It is an extremely rare number in full force.

What makes it especially rare is the fact that the number only matters if found among the following: the heart's desire, the life path, maturity number, personality, expression, or as a pinnacle cycle or essence cycle. Otherwise, the 33 will be only as effective as the 6.

The 33 happens when each of the three units – month, year and day – of birth add to 11. It also happens when the year of birth adds to 22 and the day and month of birth bring a combined total of 11. It is important to note that only very rare cases yield these. For instance, in the 20th century, there are only seven years adding to 22: 1939, 1948, 1957, 1966, 1975, 1984 and 1993.

Chapter 9: If You Born On The 5 (Fifth) Or 14th (Fourteenth), Or 23rd (Twenty Third) Of Any Month Than Kindly

READ THE FOLLOWING:

THE NUMBER FIVES

In general, Fives are active, adaptable, curious people who insist on your independence. They prefer flexible hours and will always add a new dimension to whatever they do. Fives are very good sales people gregarious and persuasive. Fives love a good deal and want to be successful. They are spontaneous and know how to take advantage of an opportunity.

They move quickly and do not brood over losses. They are charming not always too serious and love being the devil's advocate. Fives open new territory, promote big business deals, and do not except the word "can't". A wariness in your nature may make you a bit impatient and easily bored with routine. You may have a tendency to shirk responsibility.

You enjoy traveling. You may want to marry late so that you call explore first. Adventures, you need work that is challenging, risky, and different. You would be a excellent promoter being something of a ham yourself.

You are known as a good storyteller and jokester and will learn much through love affairs. You tend to use things up quickly and seek new stimulation.

You are inclined to work well with people and enjoy them. You are talented and versatile, very good at presenting ideas.

You are always on the alert, curious, and questioning and love to rock the boat. You will have a variety of jobs and will leave home early to seek your fortune, which, you are convinced in just around the corner. You see yourself as something of a hobo prince or lucky lady.

You may have a tendency to get itchy feet at times and need change and travel. You tend to be very progressive, imaginative and adaptable. Your mind is quick, clever and analytical.

IF YOU WERE BORN ON THE 14th

You may have most interesting life, studded with setbacks that cannot keep you down. You must be careful to know your boundaries. You will meet people throughout your life with whom you feel a "karmic" connection. You are talented and versatile, competitive vigorous and can be discipline when there is some short term goal to be gained. You are, very good at presenting ideas, and you are also very good at organization and systematizing.

You like to experiment and crave stimulation. You should be in business for yourself; anything to do with travel, Promotion, the public, performing and entertainment appeals you also you are inclined to work well with people and enjoy them. But often restlessness in your nature may make you a bit impatient and easily bored with routine, and rebel against it. You have a tendency to shirk responsibility.

You may have a tendency to get itchy feet at times and need change and travel. You tend to be very progressive, imaginative and adaptable. Your mind is quick, clever and analytical. You want to live, not just exist. You may have a very opinionated nature based on what you have "experienced in the past".

You have a highly visible sexual nature. You may be eccentric at times and may call for help.

You need to learn independence, self-initiative, unity and justice. Your great need in life is to achieve temperance, prudence, balance, harmony, and patience in life. You have the zeal power and motivation to make a success in anything you think to do. You are also warm and have a great deal of natural wisdom with new creative ideas. You are also the one who possess everlasting movement and tend to bring trials and dangers from a great variety of experiences. You people at times experiment for the sake of experience only. Such behavior may lead you to chaos, but finally your aim is to try for progressive change and the final joy of growth and renewal.

People with number fourteen as your number are warm-hearted and naturally creative. They are quick to learn independence, self-initiation, unity and justice. They are very single minded need a constant challenge, however, or they may quickly become bored. This is a number of attractive characteristics and they tend to attract the opposite sex. They are polite and diplomatic and have a lot of good friends. They can only think and work with one thing at a time.

They are known to possess a great deal of wisdom, which they freely share with others. If they act cautiously they can be fortunate in money matters or business transactions. If anyone gives them too many things to think of at any one time they become decidedly vague.

People of number 14 are both make progress in the material field, but when it is loneness; they are put off by friends. From it they need to get rid of. Their mindsets are negative, and this complicates the relationship.

They must have their mind set on a bed of more positive and power the strength of their good qualities. They have the tendency to be born with money greed.

They succeed in substantive matters, they carry with them the leadership skills, initiative, energy, mind, that they can bring to the acquisition of money. For the following people their spouses and friends must be very rich, otherwise they cannot hope for good relations. These people are not very sincere, and they are hard to love

On the other hand spouses of these people need to have the same materialistic. They are unable to cope with people who have a different mindset. They do not need those who do not care about money. On sexual event they are strong people, but also in the field of their.

Number 14 people are opportunists and use people according to their needs and when they are no longer needed, do not seem care for them, thus gaining lot of enemies. Being somewhat pessimistic, it is suspicious. Such people are extremists and they are falling from one extreme to another.

These people are very active and steady in their work and they have the faith to succeed in it. They will not get entangled in unnecessary update complications like the other number natives. Like a child, they freely mix with others. They pretend to speak from the bottom of their heart without hiding any-thing.

Their positive qualities: Their minds travel fast like electric current. They have the ambition to accomplish what is impossible for others to achieve. They are experts in attracting others towards them. They have excellent taste in jewelry, luxury articles and perfumes. Their negative nature: strong negative influences on other people and keep their negativities in check.

They must concentrate only on ways of improving and elevating themselves. Nobody can fully understand them. Where it is necessary, they will talk in an engaging manner. Where' silence is more effective, they keep quiet and achieve their object.

IF YOU WERE BORN ON THE 23rd

You are extremely independence, self-centered and sufficient. You may have an eccentricity for which you are known. You may be interested in art and music or new age ideals. You have an interesting way of viewing life and turns events to your advantage. Verbal expression, witty, and, at times, defiant you can be petty and critical under stress. Generally however you excel in persuasion and know what other peoples will buy. You may appear youthful a long time.

You are versatile and talented and there are few things you cannot do. You have a very sharp mind and a fine understanding of the body, which makes careers in medicine or health both possible and rewarding. It also reveals how you can tackle the problems and challenges that come your way and also how you shall grab opportunities through the passage of your life. The birthday number is very closely connected to adaptability, which makes changes easier for you than for others. Your number relates to your inherent talents and abilities in you.

You have an easy path to good relationships with the result you generally get along well with most people you meet in life. You have a gift for communication and promoting yourself. You are quite charming affectionate and sensitive. You work well with others as long as there are not too many restrictions placed upon you. You do not like to be stacked to the same place for long; you easily get restless and bored if positioned at one and same situation for pretty long.

You are quite affectionate and sensitive. You work well with others as long as there are not too many restrictions placed upon you. You do not like to be cooped up in the same place for long; you get restless and bored easily. The independence of spirit, originality, fearlessness in thoughts, speech and expressions make you a fighter by nature. Your determination, self-confidence and courage in you are added by lively thinking and vigorous thoughts, which give you great success and recognition and you, are rewarded with this magnitude prize.

You have a very sharp mind and have gifted and promoted yourself with skills of communication and speech. You possess talent in verbal and writing skills, and this leads you to become excellent sales managers. Your challenge is to be willing to start your enterprise and take adequate steps toward enlarging it to its full scale. You are orderly and patient. You have a talent for seeing both the side details of a plan and how it should be worked and unfolded.

You have creative and witty nature which makes you to approach a problem methodically and systematically. Your solutions tend to be unique. You like not to be cheated as you are talented and there are very few things which you cannot do. You keep your own counsel and have much inner strength. On the reverse side, you can be nervous and may suffer grave doubts about yourself, which you also tend to hide in front of others.

People with Number 23 need to take any life situations wisely and sporty. They must do their best to stay away from any violent conflicts. As they are enthusiastic, ambitious people, looking for spiritual satisfaction in life must refrain themselves from any violence.

Since they have a creative thinking, with sharp open-mind, and are quite imaginative and bold, this allows them to quickly implement their plans into reality. They take life seriously and firmly and they intend to take everything that is possible for them to work out

They are not afraid of any obstacles. Usually they keep their emotions under control. They are very fair and merciful, and can tolerate the other types as well, because they are quite soft and curious they develop their skills in the right direction, they make a good career. if they sincerely believe that as to what they are doing is the right thing. At times they may be somewhat nervous, but and are able to restrain their passions.

They possess many great talents. A good and harmonious relationship is quite possible for the Number 23 with two types of people: one those who will obey them, and the other who possess the powers of this kind, but the biggest appreciation they will always show for those, who really obey them..

Positive qualities: enthusiastic, ambitious people looking for spiritual satisfaction refraining themselves from any violence. Creative thinking, sharp open-mind, quite imaginative and bold.

Negative Traits: nervousness, suffer grave doubts about self, tend to hide in front of others. Avoiding many restrictions, and self-centered person

Chapter 10: Name (Or Expression) Number

The Expression number is one of the core numbers. It is even considered as the most essential numbers in the numerology chart of a person. Based on your birth name's letters, your expression number can reveal the abilities, talents, as well as shortcomings you hold. The name of a person represents his/her personal history. Whatever your history is, this will shape your future. Before parents meet their kids, they already have instincts about their kid's name. This intuition will serve as the guiding force which will pick up the personal vibrations of the child. The name that is given by your parents was actually meant for you. For you to determine your expression number, you need to write your full name. Then, add the numbers of your name. Since the alphabet is using an ascending form, the numbers used start from 1 to 9 only. The result will be your expression number. If you have encountered a result like 33, 22, and 11, do not reduce them because they are called Master Numbers.

The expression number is calculated the same way as the Destiny number (in many instances they are one in the same)

The Numbers

Expression Number 1

You're a natural leader, individualistic, independent, courageous, and ambitious. You also have the ability to influence the opinions of others. Since you are number one, it symbolizes that you are a pioneer, a front-runner, a risk taker, a warrior, a top politician, a general, a self-made millionaire, a businessman, an activist, an inventor, or a religious leader. You can also be self-centered because your personality is powerful and you sometimes refuse to see a potential weakness or flaw in your plans. You can also alienate others, so you need to control your personality if you like to maintain a good relationship with other people.

Expression Number 2

You are open-minded and friendly with a great talent and highly developed intuition. Your abilities are best expressed when you are working with others. Since you tend to stay behind power and throne, you often don't get the recognition and credit you deserve which can be frustrating. Sensitivity is the key to your characteristics. Yet, this may also throw you off balance and vulnerable to an unkind conflict or word. You get upset by various circumstances. Harmonious and close relationships are important to your happiness and can make you the best partner.

Expression Number 3

You're optimistic, expressive, inspiring and outgoing. Your personality is extraordinary and can powerfully affect other people. You inspire other people effortlessly. You are also a social person. You have great potential in arts which require you to provide creative solutions to your problems. The number three is the number of self-expression and creativity, but you have to be careful when showing off your talents. You also need to discipline yourself and learn how to focus to be successful.

Expression Number 4

You're the foundation of enterprise. Your strategies and approach to problems and life is structured and methodical. Many government officials, accountants, managers, lawyers, and bookkeepers are born with expression number 4. You are attracted to music and arts, but you typically use love as your inspiration. In terms of relationships, you are somewhat moralistic. You are trustworthy and have integrity, but you can be stubborn and rigid with your strong dislikes and likes when overruling common sense. Your obstacle is being imaginative as well as being attracted to more people who are creative with their lives.

Expression Number 5

You love change, free-spirited, love to seek out different kinds of adventure, and always excited with everything. Freedom is everywhere with number five and your life revolves around it, which is why you have many talents. You also like to try everything in your life which may lead to a dangerous experience. You can be scattered and unorganized, but you are gifted when it comes to communication. A person who was born with expression number five can be a successful politician, public relations person, salesman, minister, or lawyer. Your enthusiasm is attractive and infectious to others. You fall out and fall in love frequently and you should guard yourself against relationships and shallow feelings. The key to your success is healthy limits and self-discipline.

Expression Number 6

You are caring and loving with the potential to put others before yourself. You are trustworthy and responsible with high regards to honesty and justice. Your level of creativity is high in almost all aspects in life. However, your talents are undeveloped because of servicing to others and sacrificing your time. Since your gift is for harmonizing the opposites, you are qualified to integrate and handle contradictions. This makes you a natural healer and counselor.

Expression Number 7

You're driven by your desires for knowledge and truth. Gifted with a logical and analytical mind and has a huge appetite for answers. You have an interest in exploring mysticism, philosophy, and scientific matters. You also tend to keep your feeling and thoughts hidden. Typically, you require time for yourself. You are sometimes amazed by the depth of knowledge or lack of understanding of others which may cause you to be cynical, distant, and critical about life. Meditation, tuning in to lower or softer vibrations in life can make you peaceful.

Expression Number 8

You have the potential and power to achieve the best things. You are also competitive and whatever you enterprise, you always achieve success. Authority and money are available to you. You are a good leader and an outstanding judge. Your path requires balance between taking and giving. You may fail to obtain success if you don't know how to balance your spiritual and material aspects.

Expression Number 9

You are filled with great idealism and compassion. You are also a humanitarian and your intention is to change the world. You also realize that your satisfaction involves activities which directly benefit the public. You are not good in judging one's character, yet you have a belief that humanity's goodness is unshakable.

Expression Number 11 (Master Numbers)

You're a powerful presence, but you are not aware of your inner power. You're sensitive as well as aware. You also sense that you are not the same with others. For you to psychologically and emotionally be at peace, you should learn how to control the flow of your energy. You are dependent in relationships and highly emotional. Your love life has ups and downs. You may also find yourself vulnerable and hesitant.

Expression Number 22 (Master Numbers)

You dream huge and you dream of making a history. There's no limit to what you want to do. You have great abilities in leadership and racial identities don't matter to you. The expression number 22 characterizes those persons who realize that they need to enter another dimension. However, you are not the type to take risks because you are afraid to get frustrated.

Expression Number 33 (Master Numbers)

The expression number 33 is called the Master Teacher, but you are not just any type of teacher. You come with high expectations and you are demanding. For some people, this expression number is similar to number six which is caring and loving. However, the expression number 33 can be influenced in a negative or

positive way.

Chapter 11: Karmic Debt Numbers

MOVING RIGHT ALONG... we are! You have learned calculations, cycles, Core numbers, Life Path numbers, Attitude numbers and Master numbers, and now we enter the study of the Karmic Debt numbers where you will find enlightenment into yet another layer of how "knowing your numbers" can significantly impact the decisions you make in life.

13, 14, 16, and 19 There are only four Karmic Debt numbers in numerology. They usually show up in the birth date but can also be revealed in the five Core numbers. With that being said, the Karmic Debt number, which shows up in the birth date, is the strongest energy. Why? You might change your name, but you can never change your birth date. The birth date holds the strongest energy. Although the name is very relevant, the remedies come from name a change, which then changes the Karmic Debt number.

We all have karmic **lessons in our lives that teach us something**, but a Karmic **Debt** must be paid back for something done in a prior lifetime. Now you are asking, "What exactly does **Karmic Debt** mean?" Well, first and foremost, it is an obligation of sorts—which you must pay back. It is something you brought with you into this lifetime for the experience; and you have to pay the debt in this lifetime for the actions of a past lifetime. Obviously, the Karmic Debt numbers come with challenges, and difficulties—and although that just sounds like life itself, in this case it represents far more.

In this lifetime, look at the Karmic Debt number as one that tests and warns you. The debt numbers have to do with the meaning reflected by each specific number, so you can expect every challenge and difficulty to show up in that area. "What area?" you ask. You will understand when you read the explanation of each Karmic Debt number. Don't be overly concerned; it's not necessarily as bad as you may think; you must simply be aware…

Look at it this way: When you experience challenges and difficulties, consider how you chip away at your debt, and know it soon will be absolved. If open-minded, you will recognize in the overall scope of things, it is a good thing. Actually, your frustrations are heightened when you don't even realize you have a debt number or understand why all the challenges and obstacles in your life keep recurring over and over again.

Take your time reading through the details of each of the following Karmic Debt numbers; they may well reveal far more than you can imagine.

Karmic Debt 13

THIS KARMIC DEBT number will take on the traits of a 4.

The (1) is straight and tall… and will not bend, but may fall.

The (3) has a round bottom which conveys it will rock and roll and go with the flow.

When you put the 1 and the 3 together your challenge is represented as focus and balance since the 3 will rock and the 1 stands on a thin straight line.

KEY WORDS for Karmic Debt 13:

Focus, obstacles, and success to be reached; slacking, and using words to hurt others.

In numerology, the number 13 is not an **unlucky** number. Unfortunately, in the United States we are culturally adapted to think it is. You won't even see a 13th floor in an elevator. Other countries consider the number as filled with luck, where people reap the benefits of laying a strong foundation.

The 13 Karmic Debt number represents a myriad of past obstacles, which stand in the way of your success today. This life debt is about control: to stop judgment, look at the positive side of life, and be kind to others by first being kind to yourself. It is time to stop the "blame game" and focus on building a solid foundation to create security in your life... and in turn show love to yourself, your family and to humanity as well.

Armed with the awareness of this Karmic Debt number, it is also time to assume the responsibility to pull your life together; it is something you need to accomplish to pay your Karmic Debt.

Much of life is about overcoming obstacles, but when you carry the 13 Karmic Debt number you will encounter what you may feel is more than your fair share. If you don't pay attention to this 13 debt, you will find yourself repeating the same experiences over and over again. What will you gain? Ridding yourself of frustrations that seem impossible to overcome is what you have to gain. Ultimately, if you should surrender to this frustration, you will remain locked in the state of Karmic Debt; only to repeat it in another lifetime. If you embrace the attitude, I can't do this or if you become lazy, angry, nasty, and judgmental… simply put, you will become a (PITA), pain in the ass.

However there is hope! If you rise to the occasion and learn how to deal with the debt you must pay, you can be confident that each time you overcome an obstacle, you draw closer to the end of your payback; after all, success **is** meant to be yours.

This particular Karmic Debt number requires a lot of concentration in a specific area; you must work at it until you know the job is done, and then, with renewed awareness and strength, you are equipped to move on to life's next obstacle. Many successful people have the 13 Karmic Debt number, and when they retain the focus to achieve, they realize in the end they will receive.

There are simply no short cuts with this number; you live one day at a time, one step at a time. In order to overcome this Karmic Debt you must stay focused, have a plan, work with your cycles and timing, don't procrastinate, keep a tight schedule, keep things in order, take control and get it done.

The result will provide you with business success, financial stability, family love and security. You must admit, this is something worthy to accomplish. You brought this debt with you—so pay it back and move on!

Karmic Debt 14

THIS KARMIC DEBT number takes on the traits of 5.

The 1 and the 4 stand on a straight thin line, the (1) may fall but the (4) is balanced.
KEY WORDS for Karmic Debt 14

Freedom abused, need to learn stability and responsibility.

The 14 Karmic Debt number is about human freedom being abused. If you hold this particular debt number, you will always face challenges in your life, and forced to adapt to unexpected circumstances. If you don't adapt to these ever-changing situations, you may have issues with abuse. This abuse can include, but not be limited to: overindulgence in drugs, sex, food, alcohol and physical abuse.

The key to this debt number is control, stability, and order in your life. Being forever present and aware of all you do and why you're doing it. There will always be emotional instability in your life with this debt number if you don't stay in control; your task is to focus on your goals, dreams and desires. The feeling of freedom is what drives you. When you feel trapped, the addiction(s) can come into play because you just can't seem to get off the roller coaster ride. You feel defeated and you want to give up, so you desensitize yourself with addiction.

Flexibility is the key for this number. You must roll with the punches and come out swinging. You must embrace self-control and order. The key here remains: never give up or you will never get off the roller coaster. You will live a most unhappy life, feeling trapped and frustrated, and you will abuse yourself and possibly others.

You have the ability to enjoy the finer things in life if you are willing to work for them. "Working for them" means to keep your eye on the ball, eliminate distractions and surround yourself with people, places and things that remind you of where you are going, not where you are (because you're not staying there). You are the only one responsible for your freedom and obtaining the life you desire; no one will provide if for you.

Karmic Debt 16

THIS IS THE most difficult of all the Karmic Debt numbers. Just an FYI, this is my Karmic Debt number so I can speak both from knowledge and experience.

This Karmic Debt number will take on the traits of a 7.

A stand-tall number (1) which will stand straight and tall but can fall, coupled with a round, flexible ever-adapting and bending but never-breaking number (6).

KEY WORDS for Karmic Debt 16

Rebirth, spirit, and misuse of love that hurts others.

The Karmic Debt 16 is all about destruction of the old and birth of the new; it is also about the ego. Your "self" may have built a wonderful life but guess what? It's all on the surface. The 16 actually represents the inside—your spirit. The life experiences of the 16 are just that— experiences—good and bad.

Unfortunately, these experiences are going to come at a cost to you because the 16 is also a cleansing number. All you manifest with the ego mentality must go and be reconstructed, for the benefit of your spirit. Until the 16 reunites with spirit, nothing that is meant to be long lasting will be accomplished.

The process starts when you take control away from the ego. Ego is necessary in life, but when it takes control of the human being, the ego becomes obese (inflated) and can't move forward. Actually it can't move at all. The result is loss, and the struggle that will ensue. In the 16 Karmic Debt the ego has overtaken the spirit and controls the human. However, the human needs balance and there **is** a place both for ego and for spirit.

This number also deals with the misuse of love. The abuse in love and love affairs, each of which resulted in the pain and hurting others. You will experience the attainment and crumbling of many things in this life that has to do with love. Love of money, love of power, love of people, and love in an affair situation.

Until you learn humility, true success will not come or satisfy you. If you have experienced success you will find that it just slips through your fingers. This fall of the ego will touch every part of your life, business, work, family, lovers, friends and health. Your life will be much better for the fall, but even as you go through a particular experience, which is ultimately for your benefit, it's not going to **feel** good. But again, once aware what is actually happening, my hope is you will have learned to easily surrender… sooner rather than later. This debt number is quite intuitive, so get out of your head—which is the ego—and shift to your heart and gut to get your answers, which is where you will prevail.

When you judge others, when you treat them harshly, or you feel certain people are inferior or beneath you, you cause a kind of alienation that results in loneliness. Hopefully, along with this loneliness will come a deep knowing that your actions are totally ego-based. The 16 Karmic Debt number needs to be heart-centered… in feeling, thinking and action. This means putting the power of the ego in its place, and not allowing it to control you. When you have accomplished this shift you will begin to see that even when you are alone you are never lonely. The rich life transformations for the 16 are found in faith, gratitude and humility.

Karmic Debt 19

THE KARMIC DEBT 19 exists to assure us Karma is not always bad. When understood and worked through appropriately, its greater purpose is to help us elevate our souls and understand what we do experience.

Calculation: 1+9=10=1

You have a stand tall number (1) with a thin foundation, coupled with a (9) round top; and a bending bottom

The 0 is like a ball it will roll and move forward

This combination will help you to roll with the punches and achieve so you will receive

KEY WORDS for Karmic Debt 19

Independence, power, wisdom and spiritual knowledge; these were abused for personal gain in another lifetime.

The 19 Karmic Debt is all about learning the proper use of power. You will be forced to stand up for yourself, and learn not to assume the responsibility for things you **feel** are your business or problem. There will be times you feel you must **stand alone** in order to **stand in** your power. You will face many obstacles, difficulties and personal struggles in order to learn the proper use of this power.

Instead of maintaining a stubborn mindset, which makes you resist any help, and ultimately causes you to feel like you have the weight of the world on your shoulders... learn to take advice and ask for help. Take this to heart: you can't fix everyone and everything, and not everything you can't fix is your problem or your fault anyway.

One of the central lessons people with the 19 Karmic Debt need to learn: don't stubbornly continue to resist help. Many of your challenges and obstacles are self-imposed—you simply don't want to listen to others, or accept help or advice. You think you know it all and can do it all, but you know what? You can't! You will learn the hard way that you are not a single power.

This debt number indicates a natural leader and wants to be all things to all people. This resistance and stubbornness to ask for and receive help is the reason you may never be the leader you were meant to be. You need to learn you are the leader of **your own power**, not the leader **and power over others**. You're not better than anyone else; but you make others aware you feel you are. Controlling others puts you in prison because you assumed responsibility that's not yours. Be your own leader.

You can choose to use this power properly and be a strong independent leader or you can use your power improperly and keep yourself in the self-imposed prison. Trying to control others is a lot of work and this burden you imposed on yourself is, in fact, your prison.

Chapter 12: Common Mistakes

By now, you should already have a good grasp of the meaning of every number. It is strongly suggested that you learn them by heart. Now, it is time to learn the common pitfalls that beginners usually encounter so that you will not have to fall for the same mistakes. Remember that merely knowing these pitfalls are not enough; you should also make changes and put everything that you know into actual practice.

Neglecting your life path

You should already know that you can actively work on any number and adapt its qualities. However, do not fall for the same mistake that others do: neglecting your life path. Remember that your life path is the number that has a strong and continuous influence on your life. You cannot escape it. If you do, bad things tend to happen.

Not balancing your priority

Many practitioners of numerology get too obsessive with a particular trait, which creates a very unbalanced outcome. For example, if a person wants to add some romance into his life and works on the number 6, he would spend hours trying to adapt this number sometimes at the expense of other numbers that he already have affinity with. This is wrong because he tends to neglect the other aspects of his life. When working with the numbers, discipline is a very important factor.

Excessive quality

In numerology, harmony is important. This is also the same in life. Therefore, do not absorb a certain quality of a number to the excess. The negative qualities of a number do not just manifest when you lack the presence of such number in your life. The negative traits of a number can also be triggered when you have too much of that number. As they say, everything is in excess of what is required may turn bad.

For example, you a focus on too much material gains as characterized by the number 8, but you might miss experiencing love and romance, which are offered by the number 6.

Not expounding the meaning

Numbers are meaningful. If they were not so, the universe would not would use them as means to communicate with you. You must learn to expound the meaning of each number. There is no strict rule as to how to know the deeper meanings of a number. Of course, research can help. Another way is to have a relationship with a number. You can do this by simply learning its qualities and adapting those traits that you think can improve you as a person. Do not be satisfied with the meanings that you get from books. Just as numbers are said to be alive, you should allow them to reveal to you their deepest secrets. This, however, can only be done by experience. The key is to have a relationship with a number so that it can open itself to you.

Underdeveloped intuition

Numerology is like other forms of magical arts. You need to develop your intuition. Otherwise, you might not be able to completely understand what a number is trying to tell you. Again, one of the best ways to develop your intuition is by practicing any form of meditation regularly. Another way is to simply keep on using your intuition.

Failing to act

No matter how many messages you receive, they would not be of any good if you do not take any action. Of course, the numbers will never deprive you of your freewill. You are free to choose whether you want to follow a particular message or not. After all, numbers only tend to give suggestions. Also, when you start to live with numbers, you must be ready to leave your comfort zone. Just as the universe wants you to grow and experience the beauty and madness of life, it may tell you to do things outside your comfort zone so that you can discover something new.

Lack of faith

Many people tend to forget that numerology is a magickal art. And, one very important aspect of the pyramid of magic is faith. Without faith, you will not know the true meaning of a number. Not only should faith be found in deciphering the meaning of a number, but faith is found in the universe as well – the universe is alive and speaks to you through numbers. Also, have faith in your intuition.

Bias

Do not impose your own interpretation of a number just to get a message that you would want to have. Keep an open mind and receive the message as it is, without any prejudice or bias. Some numerologists fail to read the numbers properly because they only want to read what they want to "see". By doing so, they fail to understand what a number is actually trying to tell them.

Fear of change

Numerology can help you have a better life, but you should be ready for it. After all, numbers can only help direct your path, but it is still you who should walk on it.

Do not believe all books on numerology

It is not surprising to see stuff about numerology being categorize as for entertainment. Unfortunately, many people write things about numerology without understanding what this art is really about. Rather, they write it literally for entertainment. This is dangerous because the advice that you read may not actually be the proper way to interpret the message of the universe to you. Therefore, always take everything you read with a grain of salt. On this respect, simply remember Buddha's advice to not believe the words right away. Instead, test them, only then will you know that they are for real.

Being dependent

It is important to understand that although you study numerology, you should learn not to depend on numbers. This may seem counterintuitive, but you must also realize that you are the master of your life. Yes, numbers can help you be better, but you are also blessed with divine energy to do what you will and change the stars. Now, this step is truly extreme and dangerous. But, if your numbers become so adverse that they speak of not pursuing your dream, then you need to be careful on how to interpret the numbers. Most of the time, if numbers tell you to stop pursuing a dream that you truly love, then the proper interpretation might be that the numbers are merely warning you that the challenges that you will face will be severe. However, if you truly want to pursue a dream, then by all means, do so and let the energies of the numbers help you reach your dreams.

The above example, however, is rare to happen. It is not in the nature of the numbers to prevent a man from pursuing a dream. In fact, they will urge you more to continue and chase your dream.

Lack of spiritual maturity

No matter how many books on numerology have been written, and even if sometimes people categorize numerology as mere entertainment, the truth remains that numerology is a sacred art. As such, you must approach it with a pure soul. After all, how can you expect to take notice of the messages from the universe if you do not have the eyes and ears to understand them or if your heart is not open enough to a leap of faith and miracles? You need to be open to divine energy. Welcome it into your life by having a heart that is open to love, kindness, and faith.

Being in a rush

Do not rush the learning process. After all, there is no end to this process. As long as you exist, and even if you do not, the magic of numbers will never cease. Do not rush; instead, enjoy every new knowledge that you gain. Also, be prepared to make some mistakes, especially when it comes to interpreting the meaning of a number.

Numerology takes practice, even years of practice. Since there is no end to this study, there is no reason for you to hurry. Try to embrace every detail by heart, especially with respect to the qualities of the numbers. The more you know about the numbers, the more your soul grows attached to them, the more these numbers will reveal themselves to you – this part is something that can no longer be taught by books. In the end, let the numbers teach you.

Chapter 13: What Type Of Life-Mate Are You.

Each and every aspect of our personality is influenced by Planetary Numbers 1 to 9

Numbers are the prime causes, which create, reform, rejuvenate and reshape the trend of life. They start producing their impact on your life right from the moment of the birth and will continue to influence throughout the life.

Let us have a glimpse into how Numbers impact our behaviour as a life mate. and know what type of life mates are persons born under Number One to Nine, as we all aspire for the long-term committed relationships.

WHAT TYPE OF LIFE MATE ARE PERSONS BORN UNDER NUMBER ONE TO NINE

Number 1

A person born under the Birth No of 1 or any of its series 1,10,19, 28 is creative, inventive, confident, strongly Individual, definite in his or her views, consequently determined in all the decisions taken. No. 1 people are ambitious and aspirant to hold top position in whatever they do and don't like to be subordinated and always try to prove their point logically and assume liabilities willingly. Benevolent at heart. Prove assertive as life- partner, but very faithful and trustworthy.

Number 2

Number two people are those who are born on the 2nd, 11th, 20th and 29th in any month. Number 2 people are gentle by nature, have great power to adjust, imaginative, artistic and romantic, have marked aesthetic sense and love for music, painting and literature and enjoy traveling. In spite of being multi talented, they generally leave decision making on life partner and their financial status remains sound.

Number-3

Number three people are those who are born on 3rd, 12th, 21st, 30th of any month, are decidedly ambitious and don't like to be subordinated, are excellent in execution of commands, hard working, sincere, with a deep sense of responsibility and take good care of domestic life as well and are good at parenting. Articulate and considerate, they are equally good in professional life, but the money earned is spent by them on domestic liabilities primarily and hardly spend for their own luxuries.

Number 4

Born on 4th, 13th, 22nd, 31st of any month are non-conventional in their views and opinions and instinctively rebel against rules and regulations, are sensitive and easily wounded in their feelings. Due to their habit of indulging in arguments, generally get defamation. Their intellectual level is good, are inclined to innovations and off beat style of living and don't like to depend. They become restless at times, but never hurt feelings of life-mate deliberately. They love to socialize and entertain guests. Spending quality time with kids is a passion for them.

Number 5

Born on 5th, 14th, 23rd in any month are quick in thoughts and decisions and impulsive in their actions and have keen sense of making money by inventions and new ideas and are generally willing to take risk in all they undertake and have a calculative mind, have a deep sense of rhythm, music, dance. They travel a lot and especially foreign tours suit them better. They are very independent in their decisions, but always care for their family and children.

Number 6

Born on 6th, 15th, 24th of any month are extremely magnetic, unyielding and are very determined in carrying out their plans, have aesthetic taste, are fond of rich colors, glamour, painting, music and have a love for literature and lead a luxurious or at least a very comfortable and enjoy sound financial status fame. Love life is fine and they love to enjoy every moment of life. Good at parenting too.

Number 7

Born on 7th, 16th, 25th of any month have strongly marked individuality, artistic taste and become good writer or poets, painters and have a philosophical tinge in their work, a great leaning to occultism and are possessed with gift of intuition, are keenly interested in far- off lands. They have adjusting nature, but won't disclose their heart easily. Have a romantic temperament and know to live and enjoy life.

Number 8

Born on 8th, 17th, 26th in any month have deep and very intense nature and strong sense of individuality and firm in decision making. Number 8 people are either great successors or great failures and are interested in occult studies. They like to fight battle of life themselves and don't depend on life mate. They are very much dedicated to their professional and social commitments; hence tend to neglect family at times.

Number 9

Born on 9th, 18th, 27th of any month have generally tough times in their early years, but generally in the end, are successful due to their strong will, determination and guts. Major decisions of life, they take in independent capacity. They usually experience many quarrels and strife in their domestic life. Number 9 people enjoy the benefit of property and other benefits associated with land. Spiritual inclination of mind is greater in them.

Chapter 14: The Cosmic Clock Of Leo

The function of the Cosmic Clock is to show the monthly position of the sun in the Zodiac and its expected influence on Leo. For example, a Leo who feels a decline in energy and mood level in July will find that the reason for this is the location of the sun in Cancer in his 12th house. However, Leo will feel stronger and more powerful in August, when the sun moves into his 1st house of Leo.

Leo's Monthly Forecast

Leo
Virgo
Libra

Scorpio
Sagittarius Capricorn Aquarius Pisces
Aries
Taurus
Gemini
Cancer
July 23 – August 22
August 23 – September 22 September 23 – October 22 October 23 – November 21 November 22 – December 20 Sun in the 5th house December 21 – January 20
January 21 – February 19
February 19 – March 20
March 21 – April 19
April 20 – May 20
May 21 – June 20
June 21 – July 22
Sun in the 6th house Sun in the 7th house Sun in the 8th house Sun in the 9th house Sun in the 10th house Sun in the 11th house Sun in the 12th house Sun in the 1st house Sun in the 2nd house Sun in the 3rd house Sun in the 4th house

Note: For characteristics and meanings of the 12 houses of the Cosmic Clock, see chapter on the monthly forecast.

Leo: Relationships with Other Signs

Leo 1st house Virgo 2nd house Libra 3rd house Scorpio 4th house Sagittarius 5th house Capricorn 6th house Aquarius 7th house Pisces 8th house Aries 9th house Taurus 10th house Gemini 11th house Cancer 12th house

Example: Leo will be rewarded with fruitful cooperation from Aquarius but will likely experience criticism, judgment, and censure from Taurus.

VIRGO – AUGUST 23*rd* to SEPTEMBER 22*nd*

During one of my appearances before a forum, when I began to describe Virgo, one of the listeners from the audience cried out: "Virgo isn't a sign – it's a situation!" He was right from a mystical standpoint. The Virgin was abstinent in the past life of the soul, a situation often replicated, for one reason or another, as patterns of celibacy, asceticism, and purity in the present life of the here and now. But let's not misjudge Virgo — she can be quite exotic and sexy. For example, Claudia Schiffer, Raquel Welch, and Sophia Loren display, without a doubt, the beauty and stunning femininity of Virgo. After all, Virgo is the sign of the woman, virgin or not, but 100% feminine.

Virgo is the sign of excellence; and the aim is for 100%, as 95% is seen as failure. Nothing short of perfection is acceptable. Ingrid Bergman, Buddy Holly, Tolstoy — each one a perfectionist in his or her own field. And who can deny Sean Connery, a Virgo: "The name is Bond — James Bond."

The criticism and selectivity of Virgo can even drive an elephant crazy. Virgo sees details rather than the whole; he "can't see the forest for the trees," unlike Sagittarius, for instance, who sees the forest only. "It's All on Account of a Little Nail:" if the nail falls out, the horseshoe falls off, then the horse falls, the rider does not arrive at the besieged city, and the city is captured…….Virgo knows that miniscule details are of utmost importance. Pennies turn into dollars that can turn into thousands. For Sagittarius, in contrast, the sky is the limit and what good is a penny? It is not easy to pass through the scrutinizing sieve of the Virgo with its microscopic holes. Virgo is the nurse who will wake you at 6 P.M. sharp to administer your sleeping pill, since it was written on the order sheet; nurse Pisces, on the other hand, will love and stroke and care for you and will only forget one little detail – to give your medication.

Virgos tends to worry too much. They are professional and rational by nature and do not care for mysticism, cards, crystal balls, U.F.O.'s and the like. They prefer research and demonstrable connections between variable X to set Y – proof, measurement, validation, order, validity, and efficiency. Formal research is preferred to "energies" that cannot be seen by all. A Virgo T.V. talk-show host and critic will cool at the mention of astrology but will reveal a voyeuristic curiosity in a program about sexual practices.

Ora Namir, a former Labor Minister of the Israeli Parliament and a Virgo, could not stand the idea of unemployment and government benefits for same and insisted that everyone be found work. Work is paramount for Virgo and part of the daily routine. Virgo wants cause, theory and logic rather than speculation. Actors Elliot Gould and James Coburn are Virgos and remind me of the typical preciseness inherent in this sign. In the 1960 movie "The Magnificent Seven", the actor aimed and shot at a man riding a horse. The rider was hit and fell. To the exclamation of "Wow, that was the best shot I ever saw in my life," Coburn replied, "The worst….I was aiming at the horse…."

Switzerland is Virgo: cleanliness, order, quiet, etiquette, medicine, the Red Cross, and the Swiss watch. This has been a country of exactitude since the 12t[h] century. When William Tell shot an arrow and struck the apple on the boy's head rather than the boy, "puenktlich" said the Swiss. Right on the dot! This is the Virgo genre.

Concept of Time – Virgo has a creative concept of time and manages time and the clock precisely and par excellance – like a Swiss watch. Virgos are often time professionals and see the connection between time and management. They are proud of their accomplishments within a given time.

The dimension of time is related to children and to advertising. For some reason, there is also duality. Virgo lives in two time arrangements that are difficult to explain; however, time serves to make Virgo more youthful in behavior and appearance. Gemini is located in the 10th house of Virgo; therefore, Virgo will probably own more than one watch. Flexibility and manipulation of time are strong; and, of course, time equals information and vice versa.

Career and Work – Virgo will gain authority and managerial standing even if this was not the initial aim. There will be creativity at work with appreciation, goodwill, and publicity. An emotional connection with bosses and authorities is likely, but also disappointment and lack of communication. Two careers are possible. Work demands flexibility, information, instruction, guidance, and travel. Virgo often functions at work like two people. Possibilities are work with children and youth, communications, journalism and tell-all media. There is an ability to improvise, to invent, and to form friendships within the framework of daily employment.

There will be detachments and separations, surprises, innovations, and unexpected tendencies in connection with work. Hi-tech, computers, aviation, technology, service professions in medicine, psychology, social work, education, special education, and alternative medicine are all within the scope of possibility for Virgo.

Money – Conflict is possible among siblings, children, or young people. There could be a struggle followed by an agreement fostering harmony.

Virgo knows what "big picture" Sagittarius will never figure out: that it's all about one little nail. Virgo can profit from young people, children, and youth as well as through relationships, which, in one way, may be related to resources and money. On the other hand, relationships could be associated with losses.

Relationships and Sexuality – Virgo is associated with impossible love affairs, attraction to complicated and unusual characters, and everlasting love that unfortunately results in a loss of self. There is a feeling of missing out and the need for relationships involving dependency. Virgo men do not know how to separate emotionally and do not break up. This is a deep-seated personality trait resulting from the Pisces aspect of the love relationship, as Pisces occupies the 7th house of relationships and partnerships.

Nevertheless, there is a possibility of a partner who is practical and simple – a farmer, for example – and interested only in the day-to-day routine: stubborn and inflexible, lacking vision and imagination, a typical Taurus in the astrological sense.

There is a deep-seated need to sacrifice for and to take care of the relationship to the point of loss of self-identity. The partner may not be well physically or emotionally. This provides Virgo a hidden chaos that attempts to break through the multiple layers of logic and criticism. Virgo longs for love continuously and is prepared to give his or her all for this. There is a possibility of love for an authority figure or boss, or connections between love and work or career. Love may come later in life and may also involve restrictions, such as being in love with a married partner. Underneath the Virgo chastity and abstinence lies an especially strong and stormy sexuality with sudden outbursts. There is an attraction to younger partners and vice versa. Michael Jackson provides an excellent example of this. There is also a need to talk and express oneself verbally regarding sex.

Words and verbal expression are part of the sexual provocation of Virgo – telephone conversations about intimacy and sex, and sex at a very early age are possible. There is also a chance of bi-sexuality in the Virgo male.

Home and Family – The father is paradoxical, introverted, educated, creative, and associated with management or travel abroad. He may have traditional or very religious roots. There may be a lack of communication with him or, in contrast, a powerful love and warmth. He may experience health problems or premature death. He could be well-known in his profession, which may involve medicine or service. He is dominant toward the outside world, but inside, he is sensitive, complex, and often silent. There is a need to care for and assist the father. There is no separation from the image of the father figure; and there is a symbiosis involving dependency and sacrifice, feelings of victimization, and subjugation to the relationship. Virgo at one moment feels that the father is someone very special and at the next feels that he is a loser.

The mother is intelligent, curious, communicative, youthful, social, innovative, future-oriented, surprising and unconventional. She inspires a feeling of openness, flexibility, and ease. There could be sudden separations or nervous problems.

Siblings are difficult, introverted, serious professionals. There could be friction, jealousy, and problems involving property, inheritance, money, and feelings of revenge. Fraud and cheating are sensitive areas. Feelings of betrayal, disloyalty, and dishonesty may be present. It is impossible to separate from the connection. Siblings generally are associated with delays, deterrents, and denials; they cannot be convinced, and time does not heal the wounds in this case. Things simply go on and on. There is a feeling of something unclean – a certain degree of dishonesty, manipulation, and cycles of destruction and renewal. The final scene is often one of catharsis.

Children – The connection is difficult. Children are emotionally complex, unusual, and creative and love music. There are long periods of detachment, disappointment, feelings of betrayal, and emotional burden. Health problems, hospitalizations and premature death may be present. There must be sacrifice. Feelings of inferiority involve the children, as well as binding compulsive situations or obsessive behavior. Children are often gifted in creativity and thought processes. They may arrive when the mother is either very young or else at an advanced age. There can be a connection to advertising and management on a professional level, to secrecy or undercover activities, or to deep-sea diving.

Despite everything, Virgo will sacrifice and care for the children with devotion, feeling victimized only slightly in the relationship. It is possible that the child will feel this way. There is a need for better communication and the setting of boundaries, which are often either restrictive but sometimes blurred or non-existent.

Homes – There is a possibility of living abroad for a particular period of time. The home contains signs of travel to faraway places. Virgo desires a large, spacious, and innovative home, preferably in natural surroundings or on an upper-story. Due to the dual nature of Sagittarius occupying the 4th house, the home environment could either be fastidiously clean and neat or else in total disarray.

Virgo could profit through real estate and land dealings. There is an aristocratic feeling at home or an image that does not exactly fit that of the ascetic modesty of the true Virgo. Detachments and cutting-off are possible in connection with the home and with electricity. There is also a chance of parties, social events, studies, or group activities taking place at home.

Studies and Travel – There is a connection with money and the need to improve ones financial status and living quarters. Travel is also connected to the need to help and be of service. A prime example of this is Mother Teresa, a Polish nun and a Virgo, who spent much of her life among the impoverished of India. For some reason, a motive involving food also appears. Incidentally, Virgo, who knows how to cook, has a unique sense of improvisation; menus are often surprising and unconventional. Virgo feels at home when traveling abroad, and travels may include underdeveloped countries. Studies are serious and involve concrete areas, which may be connected with food, service, or therapeutic professions.

Self-image – Virgo's self-image is low, particularly at an early age. With the passage of years, involving work and profession, there is an increase in selfimage along with status, which Virgo feels that he does not deserve. Virgo gives but does not receive. In love – hard as well as soft, judge as well as victim – strange, isn't it? Virgo gives his excellence to others at no charge, particularly to his boss at work.

Legal situations – are connected to money and property, possibly to land and real estate, children and youth, creative interests and publicity. There is also an association with travel abroad, education, authoritative bodies, and the past.

Health – There may be sensitivity in several areas, including iron levels, the heart, the intestines, and the immune system, as well as a tendency toward low blood pressure.

Mode of Dress – Virgo's dress is solid and modest, often somewhat dowdy and ordinary. It is difficult to part with old clothes. Nevertheless, there is a display of good and refined taste.

Relationship to the Past and the Future — There could be a detachment from the past or an inability to remember. The past is connected to friends, social groups, and individuals and possibly to a better life. The future is associated with criticism, work, efficiency, and accomplishment.

Religion — Virgo views religion from an intellectual and historical point of view and could have a penchant for particular religious issues and symbols. There may be a connection among religion, love, and authority and a spiritual conception of God's love for man and vice versa.

Death — Virgo is permitted to discuss and express feelings fully in relation to death, which may be associated with younger people. There is a need to wage a constant struggle against the inevitable.

Army — Military service may be associated with medical problems, phobias, and possibly depression during the tour of duty. Virgo could be assigned to units involving secret activities, intelligence, military police, or health services. There is a possibility of self-destructive behavior during service, feelings of degradation, insurmountable competition, and compulsive situations. For Virgo, military service is associated with powerful sexual energy.

Environment and Neighbors – Virgo has a close and intimate relationship with neighbors, although there is suspicion, censure, limitations, and manipulation connected with emotions, concealment, or money. There are cycles of destruction and renewal in relationships with neighbors, which may involve insults, humiliation, and even legal matters. The situation is long range and impossible to cut off. It is reasonable to surmise that there could be neighbors who are involved in subversive activities.

Cars – Breakdowns, damage, fraud, and dishonesty are associated with Virgo's buying or selling cars. Virgo, however, holds on to a car for a long time, as it represents position and status. Also, in a version of the American drive-in, the car functions as a bedroom or a motel. As the sexual Scorpio occupies Virgo's 3rd house, the connection between sex and the car is a package deal.

Relationship to History – Generally speaking, history is interesting from an intellectual standpoint, but on a personal level, there is a detachment from the past and a movement forward. This is a paradox. In connection with personal history, there is much separation and disconnection. In a certain sense, Virgo thinks that the past is the future and that what was will be, since Cancer occupies the 11th house.

Concessions, Sacrifices, Confusions, Illusions, and Places Where it is Difficult to be Rational and Objective – Marriages and relationships could lead to situations of confusion, failure, pain, inability to separate, or the need to sacrifice. Feelings of giving up and being a care-taker are pronounced. There could be denial mechanisms and sensations of loss or missing out. Often, emptiness and lack of communication in love relationships or with children are experienced, which could be associated with the past father image.

There may be a feeling of missed opportunity in connection with personal development and creativity in the course of life. The position of Leo in the 12th house will cause situations of loss and missing out in love, or at least a feeling of such. There is unrequited love, platonic love, or impossible love situations.

Chapter 15: Tips With Numerology

Now that you know a bit about what numerology is and some of the things that it can measure, it's time to look at the tips that can help you get the most out of this. For many, there are a few things that you do need to think about when you are using this, so it's important to keep these in mind before you get started.

The first is that these aren't full absolutes. For some of these, they are inherently within you, but don't' be scared if you have some of these destinies and traits within you. Remember, at the end of the day, if you're going to use this for a big decision, you're the one with the final say on it. You should be able to see that, so if you want to make a choice in a matter, take some time to look at the nature of it, and you will then start to notice that the real meaning of things is that you're able to have a life that is worth living and also one that has meaning as well.

For many people, they take their destinies too seriously, but if you see the destiny that you have, just take a look at yourself, see if you're lining up with the destiny that you have. You might not be a person who thinks they can control the destiny that they have, but you are, so do take that into consideration before you freak out that something showed up on your life path that you're not a fan of. Often, people who are starting with this can get a bit frazzled by the sheer scope of this, but don't' worry, because you will be able to take the destiny that you have, harness the numbers, and at the end of it, get a good reading for yourself that can help you shape your ideals.

Checking up on the traits every now and ten can help you keep on a good path. From this, you can determine how your life will pan out in relationship to your destiny. Remember, at the end of the day that is what's within you, and you will start to notice that you can work your destiny into your life. Even if it's a little thing, you can use the numerology that you've learned to shape yourself.

You should also make sure that when you do this, use your full name. All too often, people will use the wrong name when looking at the destiny and fate that they have, and you will start to wonder if you're doing something wrong. Just because we might have a name change, a name dropped, or even a nickname in play, doesn't mean that our birth name isn't something that we should look at. The birth name is the name that started it all, the one that the destiny numbers follow, and it's important to realize that it's the only number that really matters in terms of what your fate will be. That's the one that determines the fate, not anything else.

You should also check with other numerologists that are out there. Sometimes, you might be confused about something, but if you're able to consult others and ask them about it, they'll be able to tell you a thing or two about it.

You should consult others as well, because they might be able to help you read into your destiny and the numbers surrounding your life. You might be shocked, but that can do a whole lot.

Finally, have everything written down and mapped out when you do this, because if you have everything listed, you'll be able to really get the most out of your life. You can see for yourself what you're getting into, the different natures of it, and the power that you have. Do that, and you'll be able to create a lasting, lifelong prediction and you can use this to help you use numbers to help with your destiny and your future.

Chapter 16: Expression Number

Your Expression number is one of your core numbers -- the most important numbers in your Numerology chart. Based on the letters of your full name at birth, your Expression number reveals the talents, abilities and shortcomings you hold in this lifetime.

Why your name? Your name represents the inheritance of your personal history up to the moment of your birth. Whatever that history is, it has shaped you into what you are. Prior to meeting their child, parents use intuition as their guiding force, picking up on the child's personal vibrations and choosing a name accordingly. The name you were given at birth is the name you were *meant* to have.

To figure out your Expression number, write out the full name you were given at birth -- first, middle and last. Then, use our guide to the right and place the numerical value below each of the letters. Next, add the numbers of your first name and reduce them it to a single digit. Do the same for your middle and last names. Finally, add the three single-digit numbers together, then reduce them to another single-digit number to reveal your Expression number. If you encounter a Master number -- 11, 22 or 33 -- in any of your reductions, do not reduce it any further.

Expression number 1

You are a natural leader, independent and individualistic, ambitious and courageous. You also possess the ability to influence the opinions of those around you. Since the number 1 symbolizes the front-runner, pioneer, warrior and risk-taker, generals, top politicians, businessmen, self-made millionaires, religious leaders, inventors and activists are often born with a 1 Expression.

You may have a tendency to be self-centered, because you so powerfully identify with your goals and ambitions that you sometimes refuse to see a potential flaw or weakness in your plans. You can also be highly critical of others, which can alienate friends and family members -- you must learn to control this tendency if you want to maintain harmonious relationships.

Expression number 2

You are friendly and open-minded, with a highly developed intuition and a great talent for working with others. Your abilities are best expressed while working with others in a partnership, rather than in a leadership role. Since you tend to be the power behind the throne, you often do not get the credit and recognition you deserve, which can be frustrating.

The key to your personality is sensitivity, yet this can also make you vulnerable, thrown off balance by an unkind word or conflict. You are far more upset by these circumstances than people without your sensitivity. Close, harmonious relationships are essential to your happiness, and you make an excellent partner: giving, thoughtful, and conscious of meeting the needs of your loved one.

Expression number 3

You are optimistic, inspiring, outgoing and expressive. Your personality has a certain bounce and verve that so powerfully affects others that you can inspire people without effort. You are a social person, yet you have to learn to accept the involvement of others in your life. You have great potential in the arts and areas that require creative solutions to problems.

Yours is the number of creativity and self-expression, but you must be careful not to scatter your talents. Your bane is that you often lack discipline and order in your life -- learning to concentrate and focus is your key to success.

Expression number 4

You are the foundation of any enterprise. Your approach to life and problems is methodical and structured. Many accountants, bookkeepers, government officials, managers and lawyers are born under the 4 Expression. You can be attracted to the arts and music, but will likely bring your love of order to any artistic field as well.

In relationships, you tend to be somewhat moralistic. You have integrity and are trustworthy, but you can be rigid and stubborn, with your strong likes and dislikes overruling your common sense and compassion. You are driven by a contempt for all that is unstable, insecure and unpredictable, which may shut you off from shortcuts and creative solutions provided by more daring people. Your challenge is to be more imaginative and attract more creative people into your life who can advise and inspire you.

Expression number 5

You are a free spirit, loving change, adventure and excitement. Freedom is the nucleus around which your life revolves, and is needed for you to bring forth your many talents. You want to try everything at least once in life, which could lead to trouble in the form of unhealthy and dangerous indulges.

Your thought process, like the rest of your life, can be unorganized and scattered, yet you are gifted in communication and could be a successful salesman, politician, lawyer, public relations person or minister. Your youthful enthusiasm is something others find infectious and attractive. You fall in and out of love frequently, and must guard against shallow feelings and relationships. In fact, self-discipline and healthy limits are the keys to your success in virtually every area of your life.

Expression number 6

You are loving and caring, with a tendency to put the needs of others before those of yourself. You are responsible and trustworthy with a high regard for justice and honesty. You are creative in all areas of life, yet your talents may remain undeveloped or suppressed as a result of your tendency to sacrifice your time and pleasure to the service of others.

Because of your gift for harmonizing opposites, you are uniquely qualified to handle and integrate contradictions. This makes you a natural counselor and healer, creating peace between opposing points of view, or internal conflicts within the self. You also make an outstanding teacher, social worker, psychologist, artist, designer, gardener, florist or farmer. But you can be successful in business too, especially areas that involve dealing with people.

Expression number 7

You are driven by a desire for truth and knowledge, gifted with an analytical mind and an enormous appetite for answers. You have a strong interest in exploring scientific matters, philosophy and mysticism, and may be drawn to a career as a researcher, analyst, investigator, inventor, technician, lawyer, banker, priest or philosopher.

You tend to keep your thoughts to yourself and require time to be by yourself, but you must guard against completely cutting yourself off from others. You are sometimes surprised by the lack of understanding or depth of knowledge of others, which can cause you to be critical, distant, and cynical about life in general. Contemplation, meditation, and tuning in to the softer vibrations in life can steer you toward peace and balance.

Expression number 8

You have the power and potential to achieve great things. You are highly competitive -- whatever your enterprise, you strive to be the best and most successful in your field. Money and authority are available to you if you are willing to discipline yourself and persevere in the face of the considerable obstacles in your path. These obstacles are opportunities for you to learn how much power lies within you.

You are a great leader of people and an outstanding judge of character. When focused exclusively on your desire for results and success, though, you can become stubborn and intolerant. Yours is a path that requires balance between giving and taking, reward and punishment, action and reaction. It is crucial to your success that you balance the material and the spiritual.

Expression number 9

You are the humanitarian, filled with great compassion and idealism -- your deepest intention is to transform the world. You realize your greatest satisfaction when you are involved in an activity that directly benefits the public good. Politics, law, environmental protection, teaching, and healing are areas in which you would succeed.

You are not shackled with prejudice; in fact, a wide diversity of people and experiences brings forth qualities in you that would otherwise lay dormant. Despite the cool, distant personality you project, people are attracted to you. But while you are a loving and sincere person, you don't often express what you truly feel. You are not a very good judge of character, yet your basic belief in the goodness of humanity is unshakeable.

Expression number 11

You are a powerful presence, yet you aren't aware of your personal power. You are enormously sensitive and aware, and have always sensed that you are different. You possess a bridge between the unconscious and the conscious. In order to be emotionally and psychologically at peace, you must learn to control that flow of energy, lest you fall into emotional turmoil and nervous tension.

You are highly emotional and dependent upon relationships. Emotionally, you go up and down with the fortunes of your love life. You may find yourself hesitant and vulnerable throughout life, careful about sharing your feelings and choosing your friends. Your challenge is to ground yourself with strength. The more you are able to call upon your inherent human power, the greater your capacity to take advantage of your keen awareness.

Expression number 22

You dream big, and dream of making your mark on civilization. There is no limit to what you are capable of, nor to what you dream of doing. You have great leadership abilities, and borders and racial identities mean little to you.

The number 22 offers those who fully realize it a chance to jump into another dimension in which your day is expanded, your capacity to create and inspire is multiplied, and your ability to perform lasting service to mankind is extended beyond the normal limits of one's life. However, you may resist taking the great risks this number presents, which can cause frustration, because you feel called to greater things. Nevertheless, your chances to be successful are good, even when you limit your efforts.

Expression number 33

The 33 is the "Master Teacher," but not just any kind of teacher, one of intensely profound spiritual wisdom and enlightenment. It comes with incredibly high expectations, and is so demanding that very, very few people live up to its status. Therefore, for most people the 33 Expression number is similar to the 6 Expression: harmonious, loving, caring and sacrificing. However, the 33 Expression will emphasize all these qualities of the 6 -- and they can be influenced in a positive way or in a negative way. When the 33 takes on a negative influence, you could actually be emotionally and physically damaging to those around you. But when positive, your ability to heal, comfort and care for others becomes a very prominent part of your makeup. You draw people toward you like moths to a flame.

Chapter 17: Warning Numbers

Remember the warning of fatal attraction between numbers 4 and 8 in my first book, "Finding And Keeping Your Crush!"?

Here a client, who has consulted me for four years with his wife, has courageously agreed to share with readers his story of how his car became 'tissue paper'. I blamed it on the set of unlucky numbers and we have the picture to prove it!

Client: Mr H

Birth date : March 29 1975

Life Path/Destiny Number : 9

Mr H vibrated to Personal Year 8 in 2010.

In my analysis, I have advised him to avoid association with 4 and 8. If not, legal lawsuits, bankruptcy, divorce, cash flow problems are all possibilities of this year. Otherwise, career wise, this is a year of ambition, career advancement, increase in wealth. If this did not happen, he is experiencing a bad luck cycle.

Mr H made an appointment to see me for a numerology consultation on September 5. In the afternoon after 3pm, I received this text message from him: "Hi Gracy, sorry pls gv mi 15min on my way. Met an accident, juz sent car to workshop:) "

I was taken aback and could not help but noticed the strange smiley. He must be traumatized but is putting on a show of Dutch courage. I offered to cancel the reading session and reschedule it to another day. To which he replied with another text message: "No worries I'm ok otw nw...keke! Car become tissue paper...LOL!!"

Mr H's car plate is 8864, the car accident happened on this date: 5 (a day of Mercury retrograde). And since September is his Personal Month 8 with 5 being his Personal Day 4 - it is a double whammy! Thank God he wasn't hurt, only his car is. I advised him to rent another car to drive or to place a talisman in his car the next time he drives it.

As you can see, when 4 collides with 8, or 8 with 8, or 4 with 4, there will be loss, even bankruptcy or mortality. Look at the appeal for a witness to a car theft by the Marina Bay Neighborhood Police Post. Note the uncanny set of numbers: 4-8-2010. That is the infamous power of 4 and 8 numbers at work.

Speaking of mortality and loss, the other warning number I want to mention is 9 and its series, the number of ending. 9 is ruled by Mars, the warrior planet.

It doesn't take much to explain the 9/11 incident, 11 being the ominous number of terrorism and 9 the fire sign associated with wars.

Beware of the warning numbers. Avoid them at all costs during unfavorable cycles like 5, 8 and 9.

Finding out what the future clearly holds is simply understanding and decoding the cycles of time. Refer to the meanings and symbolism of Personal Years in Chapter 5. Take your time to read this chapter over and over again to gain a snapshot of the Universal Year (the current year) in question.

You will discover that what you are experiencing has been predicted before its time and the events are no pure coincidence. Numerology is a lifesaver and a strangely accurate self-help divination tool.

Chapter 18: The Moon

The Moon card depicts a marshy piece of land between a river and a sea. The illuminated full moon and the dew in the sky signify the harvest moon in autumn season. A crab is conspicuously rising out of the river water and taking a watery path leading to the sea with a higher purpose.

There is a dog and a wolf on either side of the card ready to grab the crab. The towers standing aloof represent the trappings of an easy life.

The Moon is a luminary that serves as a source of intuitive clarity on a voyage to the centre of the Self. And ruled by the Moon, the Crab symbolizes the individual with a mood that wanes and waxes with the phases of the moon. The outer hard shell protects him against predators. In a mundane sense, each of us has a hard ego shell which we erect to protect the self, in the mistaken belief that it could be hurt. Beyond the water we see the path that the crab (oneself) must follow. The crab lives his life taking two steps forward and one step back. Similarly, the progress graph of those under the influence of this card will be two steps forward and one step backward. The crab walks sideways, which is how he skirts around a problem. He never takes a decision until he hems and haws over it for a very long time. Though he is tenacious, on an extreme note, one maybe is too clingy and hanging on to a hopeless endeavor. The watery path in the picture deals with direction as well as the track we choose to travel in any phase of our life (family, career, love, spirituality, etc.). Psychologically, the dog symbolizes our tamed mind which is loyal to our bidding and the wolf symbolizes our primal urges that bear its teeth at our every attempt to be conventional. Neither canine is all bad or all good - but they both are at war with each other in our minds. Hence each one is on either side of our path. One yapping at us to "do the right thing" the other growling at us to "break out and go wild." These canines lure of empty promises to pull our attention. And physically, the growling dog and the wolf signify hidden enemies, unfriendly companions, and inner conflict within oneself, betrayal and untrustworthiness. It may also represent one's habit of making demands on people and controlling situations around them. The main thing to remember is to not let the turbulent emotions of the moment crowd out your normally rational judgment. Trust our intuition.

In some numerology circles, the Moon card is also depicted as a "rayed moon" from which droplets appear to be falling like blood instead of the dew. So irrespective of whether, it is dew or blood; those who fall under this vibration have intense emotions and are easily irritable. Family quarrels and accidents may occur due to rashness or carelessness. Caution should be exercised as these people may fall prey to deceptions, heavy expenditure, financial loss and unforeseen dangers. The card of the hidden enemies and uneasiness warns you to be cautious and alert all the time. Danger, disappointment, perhaps even bad dreams or depression are caused by a hostile environment. Follow your good instincts to take steps to protect yourself from intrigue or error. In the face of change or calamity focus on the positives to ease your mind. Exercise well and take special care of your health.

Karna

Name Number 18

In Hindu mythology, Karna is one of the central characters in the epic Mahabharata, and was known as one of the greatest warriors. Karna was the closest friend of Duryodhana and fought on his behalf against his own brothers in the famous battle of Kuruskshetra. Karna fought against misfortune throughout his life and kept his word under all circumstances. Many admire him for his courage and generosity.

THE SUN

The Sun card symbolizes true contentment and inner bliss. In the picture, a boy rides a beautiful white horse, with a walled garden dominated by four splendid sunflowers in the background. Behind it all is a cloudless blue sky dominated by the sun. Cultures have worshipped the sun over the ages because it gives life. The Sun is an image of optimism and fulfillment as the dawn follows a dark night. The face on the sun is an illustration of your higher mind. The child playing joyfully in the foreground represents the happiness of our inner spirit. Think about what brings a young child joy. It doesn't have to be about fancy toys or computer games - it can be as simple as spending some time outside in the sun, playing and creating a wonderful imaginary world filled with happiness, love and warmth. This is possible only when we are in tune with our truest Self. The horse is without saddle or bridle. It is controlled without the use of the hands, either. This is a symbol of perfect control between the conscious and subconscious minds. The red flag that the boy is carrying represents action and vibration. The walled garden is the cultivated garden of mankind. There are four sunflowers, representing the four elements. The sunflowers look towards the boy instead of the sun for nourishment. They are seeking his wisdom.

In readings, you will understand the Sun Card if you imagine yourself to be a Sun God. How do you think and feel? You have total confidence in yourself. You are not cocky, but profoundly sure of your power. You have unlimited energy and glow with health. You have greatness about you and stand out brilliantly. Finally, you see and understand all that is happening within your sphere. With a name number under this vibration, the natives are gifted with a good marriage, contentment in home, material happiness, honor and esteem in the society. These people will naturally possess effective communication skills and leadership qualities. They will overcome obstacles with courage. On the lower octave these people must beware of uncontrolled impulses that may bring in material loss and failures.

Plato

Name Number 19

Plato is one classical example of the Sun tarot. He was a Greek philosopher, mathematician, student of Socrates, writer of philosophical dialogues, and founder of the Academy in Athens, the first institution of higher learning in the western world. Along with his mentor, Socrates, and his student, Aristotle, Plato helped to lay the foundations of western philosophy and science.

Ashoka

Name Number 19

Another example is Ashoka the Great. He was an Indian emperor of the Maurya Dynasty who reigned over most of present-day India and some parts of Afghanistan, Pakistan and Bangladesh after a number of military conquests. After the bloodshed Kalinga war, the King renounced war and embraced Buddhism.

Ashoka played a critical role in helping make Buddhism a world religion. As the peace-loving ruler of one of the world's largest, richest and most powerful multi-ethnic states, he is considered an exemplary ruler, who tried to put into practice a secular state ethic of non-violence. The emblem of the modern Republic of India is an adaptation of the Lion Capital of Ashoka.

Dr. Suess

Name Number 19

Dr.Suess was an American writer, poet, and cartoonist most widely known for his children's books, which were often characterized by imaginative characters and rhymes. His most celebrated books include the bestselling Green Eggs and

Ham, The Cat in the Hat, One Fish Two Fish Red Fish Blue Fish, Horton Hatches the Egg, Horton Hears a Who!, and How the Grinch Stole Christmas!

JUDGEMENT

The twentieth numbered card is called the judgment, and portrays three figures rising apparently from their tombs. Above them in a blaze of glory is a winged figure blowing a trumpet. The planet Pluto rules over this card and Pluto is said to have direct ties to Karmic influences. For many, the word "judgment" evokes some very unpleasant thoughts and images. For a few hundreds of years this term has been associated with the "Judgment Day". Actually, there is nothing to fear about this card. In fact, the judgment card illustrates the liberation of man's spiritual nature from the coffin of his material constitution. Since people who fall under the influence of this card do not have a very smooth life, they usually tend to harm themselves and others by hurtful thoughts, feelings, words, and actions. Revenge, guilt and resentment should be replaced with virtues like reconciliation, forgiveness and forbearance and repentance. Do not try to leave, ignore or forget your past experiences, but accept them. Acknowledge that your choices have repercussions. Whatever you give out returns to you, multiplied. If the essence of this card is understood, then judging the precise moment to make the right choices at important crossroads in your life will bring

Conclusion

Numerology can be a very valuable tool to assist you in understanding yourself, your family members, and your potential relationship partners. Numerology can answer the questions that you may have as to why some relationships just seem to work out perfectly, and other relationships are a constant struggle. In this book, you can discover the secrets of the differences between people. The date of birth and the name is given at birth set the stage for the rest of a person's life.

The reason that numerology has existed for thousands of years is quite simply "That it really works". There are many sceptics; however, numerology is used by millions of people around the World not only to get through their day to day lives but to foresee what lies ahead and achieve great success.

The simple meaning of numerology is the revealing of spiritual insights and the attainment of material success. The meaning of numerology can also be viewed as educated fortune telling a practical system which provides a numerical analysis of life.

www.ingramcontent.com/pod-product-compliance
Lightning Source LLC
Chambersburg PA
CBHW052203090526
44583CB00015BA/1303